ENOUGH

Stewardship Program Guide

Adam Hamilton

ABINGDON PRESS
Nashville

ENOUGH
STEWARDSHIP PROGRAM GUIDE

This book is printed on acid-free paper.

ISBN 978-1-426-70287-7

10 11 12 13 14 15 16 17 18—10 9 8 7 6 5 4
MANUFACTURED IN THE UNITED STATES OF AMERICA

CONTENTS

SIMPLE GIFTS
by Elder Joseph Brackett, 1848

'Tis the gift to be simple, 'tis the gift to be free,

'Tis the gift to come down where we ought to be,

And when we find ourselves in the place just right,

'Twill be in the valley of love and delight.

When true simplicity is gain'd,

To bow and to bend we shan't be asham'd,

To turn, turn will be our delight,

Till by turning, turning we come out right.

INTRODUCTION

Welcome to the *Enough* churchwide stewardship campaign. Our hope is that this will be a useful and effective resource for you and your church as you plan your next stewardship emphasis.

In 2007, we were preparing our standard stewardship campaign at The United Methodist Church of the Resurrection in Leawood, Kansas. This campaign is a time when we celebrate what God has done in the past year, cast a vision for where God is leading our congregation in the future, and seek to inspire people about the biblical concepts of tithing and stewardship. As we were planning that campaign, one thing became painfully obvious. There were many people in our congregation who were struggling financially. They were struggling not because they were not making enough money. They were struggling because they were living beyond their means and were saving nothing.

My team and I began to feel that instead of launching a standard stewardship campaign, we needed to help people redefine their relationship with money and begin to think carefully and biblically about where we find real joy and what our lives are really about. We redesigned that standard stewardship campaign and launched a sermon series we called *Simplicity, Generosity, and Joy*. The messages from that sermon series, along with some additional material, later became the book and accompanying video study *Enough: Discovering Joy Through Simplicity and Generosity*.

As we began to plan for the sermon series, we first needed to define the problem and ask, "What are people struggling with? What are the missteps we have made?" I interviewed consumer credit counselors who regularly work with people in our community. They talked with us about the problems they see every week and the solutions they offer to their clients. Then we began to write the sermon series based on what we learned.

I sent out an invitation letter to our entire congregation that simply said, "We have a problem: Most of us are struggling in the area of finances, and we are going to try to find wisdom and help you discover joy through simplicity and generosity." The response was very interesting. In a normal stewardship campaign in our congregation, attendance drops by about 15 percent. Often, our less committed people stay away during this time. However, we saw something very different during this series. Attendance swelled! It clearly had struck a chord with the people. Those who attended wanted to find help. They wanted a simpler, financially healthy life that would bring them more joy. As attendance grew, we realized we were on the right track.

We began to teach and to inspire with stories of what a simpler life leading to financial health looks like. Each week, we gave the people tools. One week, we handed out a mirror or window cling listing six key financial principles. Another week, we gave out key tags that had a prayer of contentment printed on them; we encouraged everyone to keep the tag on his or her key chain as a reminder of what we learned. We also used some bulletin inserts that offered basic tools for making good and prudent financial decisions, including a basic budget worksheet and a life and financial goals questionnaire. To make even more help available, we began a new series of financial management workshops that were open to the congregation and the community.

Our results at Church of the Resurrection were, in the end, pretty dramatic. We had a larger number of people turning in commitment cards than ever before in the history of our church. Individuals increased their giving significantly. People shared how the series was life changing for them as it redefined their goals and their finances. The following year, 2008, was a year in which our membership gave more than they ever had before; and it was exciting.

As exciting as that was, the emphasis was not about increasing our budget. It was about helping people to experience the life God wanted them to live and to have the kind of relationship with their money that God wanted them to have. And as they did, they simplified their lives and found greater joy.

Our hope and prayer is that our experience will inspire and instruct your congregation toward similar results. Our desire is that as you use the book, the study DVD, and the resources provided in this guide in a churchwide stewardship program involving small-group study and congregational worship, your entire congregation will be blessed as individuals and families grow deeper in faith and discover true joy through simplicity and generosity.

— Adam Hamilton

I

PLANNING

PLANNING

- ❑ Implementing the *Enough* Stewardship Campaign in Your Church
- ❑ *Enough* Stewardship Campaign Activity Schedule
- ❑ The Purpose of Multi-level Communication

IMPLEMENTING THE *ENOUGH* STEWARDSHIP CAMPAIGN IN YOUR CHURCH

The *Enough* stewardship campaign is designed to meet the needs of churches of every size and description. The key to a successful campaign is tailoring the campaign and campaign materials to meet the specific needs of *your* congregation.

A fall campaign is recommended so that stewardship commitments are made prior to the start of the New Year. The campaign itself is structured to last approximately eight weeks, with planning and follow-through taking place before and after those eight weeks. However, this time frame can be abbreviated or extended as desired. For example, you could shorten the schedule from eight to six weeks by eliminating the introductory small-group study session and having only one Consecration Sunday. Or you might extend it by adding a two-week prayer emphasis prior to the campaign kickoff. Again, feel free to adapt the program to fit your schedule and situation.

Likewise, communication can be as elaborate or as simple as desired. Simply personalize the letters and other communication tools included in this resource and accompanying DVD (note all underlined prompts within parentheses), and reproduce them on your own church letterhead or stationery. Or, if resources and time permit, use the art provided to create your own custom-made campaign stationery and other creative communications, including posters and worship banners. You may prefer a "print only" campaign, or you may want to utilize email and your church website, as well.

Even the process of planning and implementing the campaign can be tailored to meet your particular needs and capabilities. For example, you might choose for the pastor(s) and administrative staff to oversee planning and implementation, or you might involve various teams in these responsibilities, such as a stewardship team, worship team, prayer team, small-group/study team, communication team, art/design team, and video team (for creating your own promotional videos and personal testimonials). Again, the key is to make it your own. You know best what will meet the needs of your congregation.

ENOUGH STEWARDSHIP CAMPAIGN ACTIVITY SCHEDULE

August

Planning & Budget Review/Approval

Order Copies of *Enough* and *Enough* DVD with Leader Guide for Small Groups

Order Gift Items (optional)

September

Weeks 1–2

Church Newsletter Article: *Enough* Stewardship Campaign Introduction

Upload Introductory Materials to Website (*Enough* Stewardship Campaign Introduction, Overview, and Schedule; Details Regarding Small-Group Study Opportunities)

Week 3

Distribute *Enough* Books and *Enough* DVDs with Leader Guide to Small-Group Leaders

Bulletin Article #1: *Enough: Discovering Joy Through Simplicity and Generosity* (run for 3 consecutive Sundays)

Week 4

Sunday

Bulletin Article #1: *Enough: Discovering Joy Through Simplicity and Generosity* (repeat)

Enough Small-Group Study Introductory Session: "Faith in the Midst of Financial Crisis"; Group Leaders Distribute *Enough* Books to Participants (Additional groups may meet Monday–Friday)

Monday–Friday

Mailing #1: *Enough* Stewardship Campaign Invitation

October

Week 1

Sunday

Bulletin Article #1: *Enough: Discovering Joy Through Simplicity and Generosity* (repeat)

Sermon #1: "When Dreams Become Nightmares"

Enough Small-Group Study Session #1: "When Dreams Become Nightmares" (Additional groups may meet Monday–Friday)

Monday–Friday

Upload Sermon #1 to Website

Email #1 from Pastor

Mailing #2: Six Key Financial Principles Letter (on Friday)

Week 2

Sunday

Bulletin Article #2: *Six Key Financial Principles*

Bulletin Insert: My Life and Financial Goals Worksheet

Bulletin Insert: Basic Budget Worksheet

Sermon #2: "Wisdom and Finance"

Distribute Six Key Financial Principles During/After Worship

Display Financial Planning Books/Resources in Designated Area of Church (for Loan and/or Sale)

Enough Small-Group Study Session #2: "Wisdom and Finance" (Additional groups may meet Monday-Friday)

Monday–Friday

Upload Sermon #2, Six Key Financial Principles, My Life and Financial Goals Worksheet, and Basic Budget Worksheet to Website

Email #2 from Pastor

Week 3

Sunday

Bulletin Article #3: *Contentment Is Key*

Sermon #3: "Cultivating Contentment"

Distribute Key Tags During/After Worship [if using]

Enough Small Group Study Session #3: "Cultivating Contentment" (Additional groups may meet Monday–Friday)

Monday–Friday

    Upload Sermon #3 to Website

    Email #3 from Pastor

Week 4

Sunday

    Bulletin Article #4: *Personal Goals and Commitment*

    Bulletin Insert: Personal Goals and Commitment

    Sermon #4: "Defined by Generosity"

    Enough Small-Group Study Session #4: "Defined by Generosity" (Additional groups may meet Monday–Friday)

Monday–Friday

    Upload Sermon #4, Personal Goals and Commitment, Giving Guide, and Instructions for Online Pledging to Website

    Email #4 from Pastor

    Mailing #3: Letters (Estimate of Giving for Active/Lead Donors, Estimate of Giving for Supporters/Regular Attendees, Estimate of Giving for New Members, Estimate of Giving for Attenders/Non-givers), Giving Guide, Estimate of Giving/Commitment Card, and Envelope (use first class postage; must arrive before next Sunday)

November

Week 1

Sunday — Consecration Sunday 1

    Bulletin Article #5: *Consecration Sunday*

    Make Additional Commitment Cards Available

    Gift Item Distribution (Optional)

Monday–Friday

    Email #5 from Pastor

Week 2

Sunday — Consecration Sunday 2

    Bulletin Article #5: *Consecration Sunday* (repeat)

    Make Additional Commitment Cards Available

Monday–Friday

    Email #6 from Pastor

    Mailing #4: Follow-up Non-Responder Letter

Week 3
  Sunday —
    Bulletin Article #6: Thank You
  Monday–Friday
    Follow-up "Caring Contact Calls" Begin (Staff and Laity)
Week 4
  Sunday — Celebration Sunday – Results Celebration and Consecration of Next Year's Ministry Commitments
    Bulletin Insert Suggestion: Print your ministry plans for the coming year on a bulletin insert.

December — (Advent/Christmas)

January
Week 1
    Mailing #5: Pledge Confirmation/Thank-You Letter, Bookmark (Responding Members), Valued Member Survey (Non-responding Members)

THE PURPOSE OF MULTI-LEVEL COMMUNICATION

In his book *Creating a Climate for Giving*, Donald Joiner says there are benefits of using a multi-level approach to communicate to different people (Discipleship Resources, 2002). Wayne Garrett and Dan Dick, both authors on this topic, also support this concept. They acknowledge that different people hear the same information differently. Communicating differently to different people within the congregation according to their commitment levels results in:

- spiritual growth
- discipleship growth
- financial growth
- congregational growth

Let's consider some of the ways these areas of growth connect and overlap:

- In congregations with high levels of financial contributions, programs that annually promote estimates of giving result in increased giving. Eugene Grimm states that those who make annual estimates of giving usually give at least 30 percent more than those who do not (*Generous People* [Abingdon Press, 1992]; p. 49).
- In congregations that practice annual commitment programs, people give much more than the amount indicated on their commitment cards when they are informed and inspired about ministry and mission needs.
- In congregations where members are taught at different levels of their spiritual journey to grow in their discipleship and stewardship commitment, there is greater spiritual maturity and financial health.
- In congregations where members are connected to small groups, classes, mission projects, and other volunteering programs, there is increased giving of time and finances.

- In congregations where people are informed and excited about what the church is doing year-round, there is increased generosity and joy.
- In congregations that celebrate weekly in worship what God is doing, people give not only to budgets but also to specific ministry and missions opportunities that change lives for Christ.
- In congregations that have the expectation of tithing and proportional giving, there are giving goals that can demonstrate growth in discipleship.
- In congregations that support year-round, biblically based generosity, stewardship, and financial management studies, growth in giving results because of deeper discipleship.

Clearly, there is a relationship between specific, planned, multi-level methods of communicating within the congregation and growth in every area of congregational life.

Suggested Communication Target Levels

When communicating to church members regarding stewardship commitments, it is suggested to target five identifiable levels or groups:

Level 1: Less-than-actives/Lapsed Members
These members are those who have no record of attendance or giving during the past three months. They need multiple letters/contacts. Always use a return envelope if any kind of response is requested. It is suggested that they be encouraged to come back to worship but not asked to make a commitment for the coming year.

Level 2: Attenders/Non-givers
These members have attended worship in the last year, but there is no record of their giving. Because they attend but usually do not respond, they need constant repetition of message. The focus in communications to this group should be on the importance of giving to God, giving as an act of worship, steps on getting started, and sensitivity to possible financial issues. (They should receive the Giving Guide.)

Level 3: New Members
New members are those who have joined the church in the last 12 months and are developing their giving patterns. The focus in communications to this group should be

on how they can honor God in their giving and make a difference. (They should receive the Giving Guide.)

Level 4: Supporters/Regular Attendees

These members are regular attendees who worship and serve and are involved at an active level of personal and financial commitment. The focus in communications to this group should challenging them to step up toward the tithe or increasing their percentage of giving if they are not yet experiencing their goals in joyful giving. (They should receive the Giving Guide.)

Level 5: Actives/Lead Donors

Actives are the leaders who are most generous in giving their time, testimony, tithes, and special offerings as a Christian lifestyle. They are the best source for increased giving. The focus in communications to this group should be on personal appreciation, celebration of results, and the joy of generosity. They should receive a personal, hand-written thank-you note. (They should receive the Giving Guide.)

All persons in every level need to hear what a difference their giving makes and how their giving is an act of faithful worship to God.

II

COMMUNICATION

COMMUNICATION

❏ Newsletter Article: *Enough* Stewardship Campaign Introduction
❏ Emails from the Pastor (1–6)
❏ Bulletin Articles (1–6)
❏ Bulletin Inserts
❏ Campaign Mailings
  • Mailing #1 *Enough* Campaign Invitation
  • Mailing #2 Six Key Financial Principles Letter
  • Mailing #3 Letters
    – Estimate of Giving Letter for Actives/Lead Donors
    – Estimate of Giving Letter for Supporters/Regular Attendees
    – Estimate of Giving Letter for New Members
    – Estimate of Giving Letter for Attenders/Non-givers
    – Giving Guide
    – Estimate of Giving/Commitment Card

❏ Follow-up Mailings and Activities
  • Mailing #4 Follow-up Non-responder Letter
  • Mailing #5 Responding Members
    – Pledge Confirmation/Thank-You Letter
    – Bookmark
  • Non-responding Members
    – Valued Member Survey
  • Caring Contact Calls Script

(The text for all articles, emails, inserts, and letters can be found on the accompanying DVD–Rom.)

Newsletter Article:
Enough *Stewardship Campaign Introduction*

Enough: Discovering Joy Through Simplicity and Generosity

Stress. Anxiety. Fear. These words capture well the state of mind of many of us in America today. We have witnessed dramatic market losses, the collapse of the world's largest insurance company, and many bankruptcies and mergers. Every day seems to bring another piece of economic uncertainty.

A recent survey found that over three in four Americans are stressed about the economy and their personal finances. Half were worried about providing for their family's basic needs. Over half of respondents reported feeling angry and irritable, and reported laying awake at night worried about this. The report concludes that, "The declining state of the nation's economy is taking a physical and emotional toll on people nationwide."[1]

Join us in worship the next (number) weeks for a sermon series entitled *Enough: Discovering Joy Through Simplicity and Generosity*. Our nation is experiencing what many have described as the "American Nightmare." Increasing consumer debt, declines in savings, lower income growth, and a volatile stock market are all a part of our economic insecurity. We have lived in a society that tells us "you deserve it now," whether or not we can afford it or really even need it.

All of us have struggled with these issues at one time or another. They are important issues that we cannot ignore. This is why, over the next (number) weeks, we will be having a churchwide study and worship emphasis called *Enough: Discovering Joy Through Simplicity and Generosity*. During this time we will explore what the Bible teaches us about financial management through corporate worship and small group study (visit [website address] for details about small-group study opportunities). We'll hear expert advice and stories about what others have learned by working through financial challenges. Each week we will provide you with some practical tools you can use to assess your financial situation and develop a financial plan with a biblical foundation.

At the conclusion of the emphasis, we will have the opportunity to make personal commitments of our offerings to God through our church in the coming year. We will consecrate these commitments in the worship service on two consecutive Sundays (see the schedule that follows).

I hope you will join us in the coming weeks as we look at how we can manage our financial resources and truly experience simplicity, generosity, and joy.

Schedule of Events:

(Date)   Faith in the Midst of Financial Crisis
            Small-Group Study Begins
(Date)   When Dreams Become Nightmares
(Date)   Wisdom and Finance
(Date)   Cultivating Contentment
(Date)   Defined by Generosity
            Small-Group Study Ends
(Date)   Consecration Sunday 1
(Date)   Consecration Sunday 2
(Date)   Celebration Sunday – Results Celebration and Consecration of
            Next Year's Ministry Commitments

---

[1] "Eight Out of Ten Americans Stressed Because of Economy," by Madison Park, from CNN.com, October 7, 2008; http://www.cnn.com/2008/HEALTH/conditions/10/07/economic.stress/index.html.

Email from Pastor #1

Our churchwide emphasis *Enough: Discovering Joy Through Simplicity and Generosity* is in full swing! Last Sunday, our topic was "When Dreams Become Nightmares." We saw how the American Dream contrasts with God's vision, and how God's vision brings joy that the American Dream never can. If you were unable to be with us, you can find the sermon message on our website, (website address).

This Sunday, our topic will be "Wisdom and Finance." We will look closely at the biblical principles of money management and discover how they apply to our daily lives. I invite you to join us for this extremely informative and practical message. You also will receive several tools that will help you in your own financial planning. See you on Sunday!

Email from Pastor #2

We are halfway through our churchwide emphasis *Enough: Discovering Joy Through Simplicity and Generosity*. Last Sunday, our topic was "Wisdom and Finance." We looked closely at the biblical principles of money management and learned how they apply to our daily lives. We also reviewed some common pitfalls and cultural traps and discovered how we can avoid them. If you were unable to be with us, you can find the sermon message and two financial planning worksheets on our website, (website address). And be sure to ask for your Six Key Financial Principles mirror cling, which was distributed to the congregation.

This Sunday our topic will be "Cultivating Contentment." If you ever feel a strong desire to have more, or if you ever look at your surroundings and feel overwhelmed by the sheer volume of things, then you don't want to miss this message! We will address head-on our human tendency to accumulate possessions and wealth and learn how to consciously change our ways. We also will be handing out a special tool that will help us to re-focus daily on contentment and simplicity. I hope you will join us!

Email from Pastor #3

Our churchwide emphasis *Enough: Discovering Joy Through Simplicity and Generosity* is nearing its conclusion. Last week, we talked about "Cultivating Contentment." In our small groups and our corporate worship, we addressed head-on our human tendency to accumulate possessions and wealth, and we discovered how to consciously change our ways. If you were unable to be with us, check out the sermon message on our website, (website address). (OPTIONAL: Also, be sure to ask for your contentment key tag, which was distributed to the congregation.)

This Sunday brings our final topic in the series: "Defined by Generosity." What defines your life? Is it wealth? Belongings? Faith? Many of us live with a scarcity mentality, worried that we must gather and hoard as much as possible, saving for some imagined "rainy day." Or we focus on self-gratification. But the Bible promises both God's blessings and joy for those who choose to live another way. During the service we will take action to change our lives by setting five specific personal goals to work toward over the next year. Then, on the following two Sundays, we will consecrate our gifts to the ministry of our church for the coming year.

I urge you to join us this Sunday as we learn how to live a new way—as people who are defined by generosity and who experience true joy.

Email from Pastor #4

Last Sunday concluded our churchwide study and worship emphasis called *Enough: Discovering Joy Through Simplicity and Generosity.* The final topic of our series was "Defined by Generosity." We considered the futility and emptiness of accumulating and hoarding possessions and wealth, and we saw that God promises blessings and joy to those who choose to live a life of generosity and self-sacrifice. We also took action to change our lives by setting five specific personal goals to work toward over the next year. If you were unable to be with us, you can find the sermon message and goals worksheet on our website, (website address).

This week you will be receiving an estimate of giving or commitment card in the mail. On a practical level, we ask our members to turn in estimate of giving cards each year so that our Finance Committee is able to set an accurate ministry budget for the coming year. This allows us to make the most of every dollar given to the church. On a personal level, the commitment card is an opportunity for you to spend time in prayer and reflection, considering what offering you would make to God through our church in the coming year. Please be watching for the mailing. Then fill out the card and bring it with you to worship this week for Consecration Sunday (date). We also will have a second Consecration Sunday on (date) to ensure that everyone is able to participate. (If you choose, you can pledge online at (website address).) I hope you will be able to join us for one or both of these meaningful services as we celebrate and consecrate our gifts to the ministry of our church for the coming year.

Email from Pastor #5

This Sunday, we will have another opportunity to consecrate our commitments of giving for the coming year. If you were unable to attend last week's service or did not bring forward your estimate of giving for some reason, I invite you to do so this week. If you have misplaced your commitment card, additional cards will be available in (location). I hope you will join us for this meaningful time of commitment and celebration. My prayer is that you will come to experience the joy that comes from knowing that your giving honors God and changes lives!

Email from Pastor #6

These past (number) weeks have been such a meaningful time in the life of our congregation. We have explored how we can manage our financial resources and truly experience simplicity, generosity, and joy. And we have responded to all that we have learned by setting personal goals and making commitments. On the previous two Sundays, we have consecrated our commitments of giving for God's work through our church.

If you have already made your estimate of giving, thank you. If you have not yet had an opportunity to do so, it's not too late. Simply drop your commitment card in the mail, bring it by the church office, or put it the offering plate during any worship service. If you need another card, extras are available at (location).

We are grateful for your financial support of our church. Your giving in the coming year will make a difference in the lives of children, youth, and adults in our church, as well as in the lives of people everywhere we are in mission and ministry in the world.

Bulletin Article #1

Enough: Discovering Joy Through Simplicity and Generosity

On Sunday, <u>(date)</u>, we will begin a churchwide study and worship emphasis called *Enough: Discovering Joy Through Simplicity and Generosity*. Over a period of <u>(number)</u> weeks, we will look at some of the financial challenges facing us as a nation and examine our own spending, saving, and giving habits. In addition to exploring biblical principles of financial management, we will learn ways to assess our financial situation and develop a financial plan that will allow us to experience the true joy that comes through simplicity and generosity. At the end of the emphasis, we will have the opportunity to make personal commitments of giving for the coming year. We will consecrate these commitments on Sunday, <u>(date)</u>, and Sunday, <u>(date)</u>. Visit our website <u>(website address)</u> for more information, including details about small-group study opportunities during this time.

Bulletin Article #2

Six Key Financial Principles

Today in worship we will look closely at biblical principles of money management and learn how they apply to our daily lives. We will review some common pitfalls and cultural traps and discover how to avoid them. We also will receive a reminder of the Six Key Financial Principles. (Hint: This useful tool, which is designed for all of us, can be especially helpful in training youth and young adults as they begin to develop lifelong habits in personal finance.) We hope you will take time this week to read these principles and Scriptures. They will make a great table devotional for you and your family. By practicing these biblical principles, all of us can find greater simplicity, contentment, generosity, and joy for our lives. Also, be sure to check out the financial management resources on display today in <u>(location)</u>.

Bulletin Article #3

Contentment Is Key

Do you have a tough time separating "wants" from "needs"? Do you sometimes feel consumed by the desire to have more? Do you ever look at your surroundings and feel overwhelmed by the sheer volume of things? When is enough, enough? Today in worship, we will release these burdens, address our human tendency head-on, and learn how to consciously change our ways. (OPTIONAL: We also will distribute a special tool to encourage you in your pursuit of contentment: contentment key tags. Each key tag has a prayer of contentment printed on it. We encourage you to keep the tag on your key chain as a daily reminder to re-focus on contentment and simplicity.)

Bulletin Article #4

Personal Goals and Commitment

What defines your life? Is it wealth? Belongings? Faith? Many of us live with a scarcity mentality, worried that we must gather and hoard as much as possible, saving for some imagined "rainy day." Or we focus on self-gratification. But the Bible promises both God's blessings and joy for those who choose to live another way. During today's service, we will take action to change our lives by setting five specific personal goals to work toward over the next year. We invite you to complete a "Personal Goals and Commitment" card and place it in your Bible for your personal reference in the coming year.

One of these five commitments is your estimate of giving for the coming year. This week, you will be receiving an estimate of giving commitment card in the mail. On a practical level, we ask our members to turn in estimate of giving cards each year so that our Finance Committee is able to set an accurate ministry budget for the coming year. This allows us to make the most of every dollar given to the church. On a personal level, the commitment card is an opportunity for you to spend time in prayer and re-flection, considering what offering you would make to God through our church in the coming year. Please be watching for the mailing; then fill out the card and bring it with you to worship next Sunday. You also can pledge online at (website address).

Bulletin Article #5

Consecration Sunday

Today is Consecration Sunday. In our worship service, we will have the opportunity to consecrate our personal commitments for the coming year. You should have received an estimate of giving commitment card in the mail. If you did not receive one or you forgot to bring it with you today, additional cards are available in (location). We invite you to prayerfully consider what your offering to God through our church will be in the coming year, fill out a card, and bring it forward at the conclusion of the worship service.

Bulletin Article #6

Thank You

Over the past few weeks, we've been looking at what the Bible teaches us about financial management. We've considered how we make and spend money, how we deal with debt, and how we save and invest for the future. We've examined how God wants us to relate to our money and earthly possessions, and we've explored what it means to live a life of gratitude and contentment. We have studied and worshipped . . . and we have responded!

On two Consecration Sundays, we received more than (number) personal commitments for the coming year. Thank you for prayerfully considering what offering you will make to God through our church in the coming year. Your gifts are an act of worship and an investment in opportunities for God to work through us. Our prayer is that you will find greater contentment and simplicity in your life as you put God first in your giving and your living. May we all experience the joy that comes from knowing that our gifts honor God and change lives!

(Bulletin Insert/Sermon #2)

My Life and Financial Goals Worksheet

How would you define or describe your life purpose?

What are three goals that can help you to achieve this life purpose?

What are some financial goals that can help to support your life goals and purpose?

Short-term financial goals (next 12 months):
1.

2.

Mid-range financial goals (2–5 years):
1.

2.

Long-term financial goals (5 years to retirement):
1.

2.

(Bulletin Insert/Sermon #2)

Basic Budget Worksheet

Item	Actual %	Suggested %*	Plan for next 12 months
Housing		25–35%	_____
Transportation		10–15%	_____
Charitable Gifts		10–12%	_____
Food		5–15%	_____
Saving		5–10%	_____
Utilities		5–10%	_____
Medical/Health		5–10%	_____
Debt		5–10%	_____
Clothing		2–7%	_____
Miscellaneous		12–23%	_____

*These percentages are adapted from Dave Ramsey's *The Total Money Makeover* (Thomas Nelson, 2007).

(Bulletin Insert/Sermon #4)
Personal Goals and Commitment

ENOUGH STEWARDSHIP CAMPAIGN

During the past few weeks, we have examined some of the financial challenges facing us as a nation, and we have looked at our own spending, saving, and giving habits. We have examined the biblical principles of financial management, and we have learned about ways to assess our financial situation and develop a financial plan that will allow us to experience the true joy that comes through simplicity and generosity. Now, on this Consecration Sunday, I ask God's blessing of my commitment to these financial goals for the upcoming year.

My Personal Goals and Commitment for (Next Calendar Year)

1. I will thank God daily for all my blessings. My goal for daily Bible reading and prayer is _____ days each week.
2. I will seek contentment and simplicity and live within my means. My spending goal is _____.
3. I will seek freedom from the bonds of credit and debt. My debt reduction goal is _____.
4. I will seek to wisely manage the gifts God has given me, investing and saving for the future. My saving goal is_____.
5. I will worship God each week by the giving of my tithes and offerings. My estimate of giving for (next calendar year) is

   _____.

Lord, *I present this commitment to you, acknowledging that everything I have and everything I am is a gift from you. I pray that you will grant me wisdom and strength in the coming year, and that you will bless and use the gifts that I humbly present to you.* **Amen.**

For personal use. Place in your Bible for reference in the coming year.

(Mailing #1)

Enough Stewardship Campaign Invitation

Dear Friends,

I really hope that you will join me in worship in the coming weeks for a church-wide study and worship emphasis entitled *Enough: Discovering Joy Through Simplicity and Generosity.* Our nation is experiencing what many have described as the "American Nightmare." Increasing consumer debt, declines in savings, lower income growth, rising housing costs, and a volatile stock market are all contributing to economic insecurity. We live in a society that tells us "you deserve it now," whether or not we can afford it or really even need it.

I'm sure we've all struggled with these issues at one time or another. I know that I have. Beginning next weekend, we are going to explore what the Bible teaches us about financial management. We'll look at what others have learned by working through financial challenges and watch some informative video clips. Each week I'll be providing you with some tools you can use to assess your financial situation and develop a financial plan with a biblical foundation.

These are important issues that we cannot ignore. I hope you will join me as we look at how we can manage our financial resources and truly experience that God is "Enough."

In Christ,

(This invitation to the sermon series can be presented as a letter or as a brochure. Please see the example mailing from Church of the Resurrection titled Invitation.pdf in the Examples folder on your DVD-Rom. In the example, this text is presented with art in a four-panel card. Text for the invitation to the sermon series is located in the Other Print Pieces folder on your DVD-Rom.)

(Mailing #2 / with Six Financial Principles)
Six Key Financial Principles Letter

(date)

Dear (church name) Member:

Last Sunday our congregation received the enclosed Six Key Financial Principles cling for your window or mirror. ((If you received a cling in worship that day, please share the one enclosed with a friend!) OR (If you did not receive one in worship that day, please come by the office. We have one for you.)) Please read these principles and Scriptures as a family. By practicing these biblical principles, all of us can find greater simplicity, contentment, generosity, and joy for our lives.

(Church name) would like to help you with this part of your spiritual life in the coming year. We will offer Sunday morning classes and small-group opportunities designed to help you with your finances. Please visit our website at (website address) to register or request more information about these study opportunities. With God's help, everyone can save more and give more by eliminating waste and reducing debt.

On Sunday, (date), the sermon will be "Cultivating Contentment." We live in a society full of economic problems that result from materialism. This message will offer practical and biblical help for the financial issues that challenge and stress so many of us. In Matthew 6:19-20, 24 we read these words, "Do not store up for yourselves treasures on earth. . . . store up for yourselves treasures in heaven. . . . You cannot serve both God and Money" (NIV). You will hear a message on how to de-clutter your life, work toward developing contentment, and learn God's will for our lives in the area of finances.

On Sunday, (date), we will have the final message in this sermon series: "Defined by Generosity." We will be distributing commitment cards for you to record your personal commitment for the coming year. The following Sunday, (date), will be our first Consecration Sunday. In worship we will bring our commitment cards forward and consecrate our personal commitment. We will have a second Consecration Sunday on (date) to ensure that everyone has the opportunity to participate in this meaningful service.

This year more than (number) households returned a commitment card as a witness of giving to God and as a way to plan their giving for our ministry. We hope and pray to increase the number of households that will take a step out in faith and return a commitment card for God's ministry and mission at (church name) in (next calendar year).

Join us in worship as we celebrate and consecrate our gifts to the ministry of our church in the coming year. We can live as people of hope, learning how to live with simplicity, contentment, generosity, and true joy!

In Christ,

(If you are not using the Six Financial Principles cling, this letter could also read, in the first paragraph:

Last Sunday our congregation reviewed the Six Key Financial Principles. In case you missed it, we are sending them to each household. Please take time to read these principles and Scriptures. They will make a great table devotional for you and your family. By practicing these biblical principles, all of us can find greater simplicity, contentment, generosity, and joy for our lives.

1. Pay your tithe and offering *first*.
2. Create a budget and track your expenses.
3. Simplify your lifestyle (live below your means).
4. Establish an emergency fund.
5. Pay off your credit cards, use cash/debit cards for purchases, and use credit wisely.
6. Practice long-term savings and investing habits.

Mailing #3 Estimate of Giving Letters

The third mailing follows the invitation to the series and the Six Key Financial Principles letter. It is sent after the fourth sermon "Defined by Generosity" and before the first Consecration Sunday and includes three important components:

- A letter designed especially for each of four groups: lead donors, supporters, new members, or non-givers.
- A Giving Guide, which helps each household think through the reasons to give, expectations, and benefits of turning in a commitment card.
- A Commitment Card

Text for the letters, the Giving Guide, and the Commitment Card follow on the next pages and can also be found on the DVD-Rom.

Thank-You and Recognition Gifts

Each of the letters for donors and new members provides a place to describe a thank-you gift. At The United Methodist Church of the Resurrection, Adam Hamilton and his team have tried several things. In this series, a coffee mug was given to each person who turned in a commitment card—even if a card was turned in without a dollar commitment. This small recognition of the community was well received.

A new gift tradition has now been launched at the Church of the Resurrection for new members as a way to encourage and recognize their first commitment. Each new member who turns in a commitment card receives a copy of the New Interpreter's Study Bible from the church. It is a more expensive gift, but it honors this first participation and commitment from new members in a significant way and sends a clear message of the importance of the commitment.

(Mailing #3)
Estimate of Giving Letter for Actives/Lead Donors

(date)

Dear (church name) Member (or Personalize),

I'm writing this letter to those members who are among our top (number) donors to simply say thank you. Together, you are responsible for (dollar amount) of our giving in (current calendar year) and without your support, our church's ministry could not happen.

Thanks to you, we've welcomed over (number) children, youth, and adults into the membership of the church in (current calendar year). Your offerings helped us teach more than (number) children in Sunday school and other children's programs. You helped us minister to more than (number) teenagers. By your support, you enabled us to provide missions support through our denomination and our mission partners here in (city/community); you allowed us to offer pastoral care and discipleship ministries to more than (number) adults, and so much more.

I am guessing that many of you receiving this letter are already giving 10 percent of your income—the biblical tithe. Some of you already give more than a tithe. To you I simply want to say, "Great job!" This is a milestone and an expression of your faith. If you are not yet tithing, I'd like to invite you to take a step in that direction. You've already shown yourself to be a generous giver. You might look to see what it would take to move to tithing. If you can't take the step all in one year, try increasing by 1 percent each year.

For me (and spouse's name, if applicable), tithing is one of the great blessings in life. Some years ago I/we began stretching beyond the tithe, and that, too, has been a meaningful part of my/our life. Each spring as I/we prepare my/our income and giving statements for income tax preparation, I/we find great joy in knowing that I/we gave God my/our tithes and offerings.

Enclosed you will find a "Giving Guide" that can help you as you consider your commitment for (next calendar year), an estimate of giving commitment card, and an envelope. This Sunday, (date), we'll be returning the commitment cards at the end of the worship service. Please take a few minutes to pray about your giving for next year. Then fill out your card and bring it with you to worship this weekend. (You may want to consider the option for automatic giving. That will help you to never fall behind in your giving. It also will help the church by ensuring that whether you are in town or out of town, your offerings will continue.) If you would rather fill out your card online, you can do so by going to (website address).

Again, thank you for all that you do to make possible the ministry of this church. You make a difference here!

In Christ,

P.S. Be sure to stop by this weekend, after you've turned in your estimate of giving card, to pick up your (gift item)—our way of saying thank you for turning in your card.

(Mailing #3)

Estimate of Giving Letter for Supporters/Regular Attendees

(date)

Dear (church name) Member,

This Sunday, (date), is the time we ask our members to return their (next calendar year) estimate of giving cards as we make plans for our ministry for the coming year. It will be a great and inspiring weekend in worship, and we'll be giving each household that returns their estimate of giving card a (gift item) as an expression of thanks for your continued support of the ministry.

I want to remind you why we ask our members to turn in estimate of giving cards each year, and to offer a specific invitation to you.

On a very practical level, we ask you to turn in an estimate of giving card so that our Finance Committee is able to set an accurate ministry budget for the coming year, making the most of every gift. On a personal level, the return of the estimate of giving card invites you to spend time in prayer and reflection, considering what your offerings should be for the coming year. I (and spouse's name, if applicable) look at what my/our expected income is going to be in the coming year, and I/we revise my/our giving based upon that figure. I/We give the first 10 percent of my/our income to the church as a tithe. Above that, I/we give other offerings to the church and to various charities and mission projects.

You may already practice tithing—giving 10 percent. If you do, I want to commend you. If you are not yet tithing, I'd like to invite you to consider taking a step toward tithing this year. Take a look at your current giving, determine what percentage of your income you are currently giving as an offering to God, and consider raising that amount by at least 1 percentage point. This is how most people begin to tithe—by gradually increasing their giving until they hit the goal.

We are grateful for your financial support of the church. Your giving this year has made a difference in the lives of children, youth, and adults in our church, as well as in the lives of people everywhere we have been in mission and ministry in the world.

Enclosed you will find a "Giving Guide" that can help you as you consider your commitment for (next calendar year), an estimate of giving commitment card, and an envelope. Please pray about your giving, and take a moment to reflect upon what offering you would make to God through our church in the coming year. Then bring the card with you to worship this weekend. You also can pledge online at (website address).

Again, thank you for your support of God's work here at (church name)!

In Christ,

(Mailing #3)
Estimate of Giving Letter for New Members

(date)

Dear (church name) Member,

I'm writing to each of our members who joined this year to let you know that this Sunday, (date), is the time when we invite every member to return their estimate of giving card for (next calendar year). There are two reasons we ask each member to fill out and return these cards each year. First, this allows the church to accurately plan for our ministries for the coming year, developing our ministry budget based upon what our members tell us they plan to give. Second, the act of filling out a card is a way of inviting each member to prayerfully set a goal for giving for the coming year.

For me (and spouse's name, if applicable), this is an important decision each year, and one that I/we make as an expression of my/our faith and commitment to Christ and an investment in the work of the church. I/We know that my/our giving is a way of furthering the mission and vision of the church. By means of our giving—yours and mine/ours—(number) new people have joined the church so far this year, many of whom have made a new or renewed commitment to Christ. By our offerings we have helped more than (number) children and over (number) teenagers to grow in their faith. Through our offerings we provided pastoral care, nursing home visits, discipleship opportunities, and hundreds of other ministries in the church. And by our offerings we provided over (dollar amount) to missions causes outside the walls of our church.

I am including three items in this envelope: A "Giving Guide" that can help you as you consider your commitment for (next calendar year), an estimate of giving commitment card, and an envelope. I invite you to pray about the commitment you would make to Christ for the coming year and then bring your card with you to worship this weekend. As a small token of our thanks, we'll be giving a (gift item) to each family that returns their card.

My hope and prayer is that your giving is a source of blessing and joy in your life.

In Christ,

(Mailing #3)
Estimate of Giving Letter for Attenders/Non-givers

<u>(date)</u>

Dear <u>(church name)</u> Member,

This Sunday, <u>(date)</u>, is the time when we invite each member household to return a commitment card to the church sharing their financial commitment for the coming year. Our records indicate that you have not given during this current year, and for that reason I wanted to touch base with you and give you a special invitation.

Some receiving this letter give in December, and if that is you, I want to thank you, in advance, for your gift.

Some receiving this letter are struggling financially and not in a position to give. My word to you is simply that we care, and if there is any way we can be of support to you—by praying with or for you, talking with you, or providing other help, please contact us at <u>(phone number)</u>.

Some receiving this letter may not have given this year because of some disappointment with the church. If there is any place where we have missed the mark, we'd like to know that by receiving a note using the enclosed envelope. Our hope is to be blessing in your life and we'd like a chance to improve our ministry.

I <u>(and spouse's name, if applicable)</u> give to the Lord for several reasons. <u>I/We</u> give as an expression of thanks and praise to God for the blessings in <u>my/our</u> <u>life/lives</u>. <u>I/We</u> give because <u>I/we</u> want to help support God's work through our church. And <u>I/we</u> give because, in the Scriptures, God asks us to give. <u>I/We</u> give to a host of other causes, but <u>my/our</u> first offerings—<u>my/our</u> tithe—goes to the church to honor God and support the work of the ministry. <u>I/We</u> <u>am/are</u> blessed and feel joy in honoring God in this way.

For the coming year, if you are able, I'd like to invite you to make a pledge of some kind, giving an amount that you feel in your heart God would have you give. I think you will find that you are blessed by your giving. Enclosed you will find a "Giving Guide" that can help you as you consider your commitment of giving and an estimate of giving commitment card. Please return your card on Sunday, <u>(date)</u>. We need to hear from every active member, regardless of the amount of his or her estimate of giving. Even if you can't or choose not to give, please let us know this. This will save us on follow-up contacts and letters.

I am grateful that you are a member of the church and wish you God's blessings in the coming year!

In Christ,

(Mailing #3)

Giving Guide
Enough Stewardship Campaign

This year we invite you to celebrate the joy of generosity as you offer your estimate of giving card for <u>(next calendar year)</u>. We encourage you to find greater contentment and simplicity in your lives as you put God first in your giving and living and to experience the joy that comes from knowing our gifts honor God and change lives. Our challenge as members is to find ways to grow deeper in our faith. One way to do this is to offer our financial blessings to God through our tithes and offerings. Through these gifts, we invest in God's vision and purpose and create an opportunity for God to work through us. Our gifts to God each week are an act of worship; and our offerings are vitally necessary to change lives, transform communities, and renew mainline churches.

Why is giving important?

The Bible has much to say about wisdom and finances, with 2,300 verses that tell us to be generous and good stewards of our resources. Jesus taught generosity and sacrifice. He demanded that his followers serve not wealth but God, and in the parable of the talents he taught that God will hold us each accountable for what we do with all our earthly possessions.

What is expected of me?

The Bible teaches us to give a tithe, or the first 10 percent of what we earn, to God and the church's work. For some, giving one tenth is a very difficult goal. For others, it is the starting point, and their giving far exceeds 10 percent. The important thing is that you start somewhere, that your giving be in proportion to your income, that your giving reflects an appropriate offering to God given your means, and that your offerings express both your desire to serve the Lord and your investment in God's work. Begin by determining what percentage of your income you are giving to God. If you are not yet tithing, consider taking a step toward tithing this year. For example, if you now give 3 percent of your income, consider increasing your gift to 4 percent, and add 1 percent each year until you reach the tithing goal. Our prayer is that everyone will grow in his or her faith through giving financially to the ministries of the church and experience the joy and blessings that come from financial generosity.

Everything we have belongs to God.

"A tithe [tenth] of everything from the land, whether grain from the soil or fruit from the trees, belongs to the LORD; it is holy to the LORD." —Leviticus 27:30 (NIV)

Why do I need to return an estimate of giving card?

There are two reasons why it is important that every member of our church family return an estimate of giving card. First, the process of prayerfully asking God to guide your decision and then making a commitment to serve the Lord with your financial gifts is an act of worship, an expression of gratitude and praise to God. Second, and on a more practical note, your commitment allows our church to budget and better plan for our ministries, key objectives, and mission outreach programs.

What if financial hardship prohibits me from making a commitment this year?

Don't let your inability to give at this time keep you from worship. Remember that God honors your faithfulness and that your acceptance at (church name) is not based upon your capacity to give. We ask that everyone return an estimate of giving card even if it is a limited financial commitment at this time. You can always increase or decrease your commitment if your situation changes by calling the church. Also, be sure to let our pastoral staff know of your situation so that they can pray for and support you during any difficulty. We also offer classes to assist members to become better managers of all that God gives them. For information, call (name) at (number) or email (email address).

Because we reap what we sow.

"The point is this: the one who sows sparingly will also reap sparingly, and the one who sows bountifully will also reap bountifully." — 2 Corinthians 9:6

Why do I need to turn in a new commitment card each year?

Financial situations change from year to year, and if we are growing in our faith, our annual commitment should likewise reflect that giving growth. Each year, our church budget is based upon the growing commitments of our congregation.

Should I use Electronic Funds Transfer?

Electronic Funds Transfer (EFT) is the easiest, most cost-effective giving option for both you and the church. With EFT, you can reinforce your commitment to give your tithes and offerings to God first, before anything else. One easy step each year guarantees that the church will receive your gifts on a regular basis, even if you are out of town or you forget one week. And on a practical note, EFT reduces the need for additional staff to process offerings. If you choose this option, you must return an estimate of giving card each year authorizing the electronic funds transfer. Complete the EFT information and attach a voided check for the account you will use. For more information contact us at (phone number).

To whom much has been given...

"From everyone who has been given much, much will be demanded; and from the one who has been entrusted with much, much more will be asked." — Luke 12:48 (NIV)

(This Giving Guide accompanies the letter and estimate of giving card. See the example mailing from Church of the Resurrection titled Giving Guide.pdf in the Examples folder on your DVD-Rom. In the example, quotes from church members are also included.)

(Mailing #3)

Estimate of Giving/Commitment Card

Name (Please Print) _____

Address _____

City _____ State_____ Zip _____

Email _____

Home Phone _____

__ **Yes! I/We will support (church name) in the year (next calendar year).**

Choose One:

$_____ weekly for 52 weeks

$_____ semi-monthly for 24 periods

$_____ monthly for 12 months

$_____ as follows _____

Signature _____ Date _____

__ I/We would like information on how to provide for (church name) in my/our will.

Electronic Funds Transfer Authorization

Please indicate the frequency of the automatic draft.

❏ Weekly—Withdrawn on Mondays

❏ Semi-Monthly—Withdrawn **first** and **third** Monday of each month

❏ Monthly—Withdrawn **first** Monday of each month

❏ Monthly—Withdrawn **third** Monday of each month

_____ Use (current calendar year) bank account information currently on file.

OR

_____ Attach a voided check for the account from which withdrawals will be made. Withdrawals will begin January (next calendar year) unless otherwise specified.

Note: *All withdrawals will be on the indicated day unless it is a non-banking business day in which case the withdrawal will take place on the next banking business day.*

(Mailing #4)
Follow-up Non-responder Letter

<u>(date)</u>

Dear <u>(church name)</u> Member,

As pastor of <u>(church name)</u>, I get to hear story after story of how our church is changing lives, transforming our community, and renewing other churches. Your support makes ministry possible.

I am writing to all members who have yet to return their annual stewardship estimate of giving cards to encourage you to return your card as soon as possible. Receiving your <u>(next calendar year)</u> estimate of giving helps make it possible for us to budget, plan, and provide appropriate resources for our ministries. I am grateful for so many who support ministry at <u>(church name)</u>, and I invite you to join us by returning your estimate of giving card.

My hope is that this commitment will also be an important step in your faith. Generosity is a personal act of worship where we express our gratitude to God and experience God's blessings and joy.

Whenever I send a letter like this, I am aware that some families are facing difficult financial times. If your finances are uncertain, a 10 percent tithe may not be possible. So, I encourage you to estimate whatever percentage you realistically think you will be able to contribute in support of the church's ministries. As your situation changes throughout the year, you can easily adjust your estimate of giving up or down with a phone call or email.

You may return your estimate of giving card in the offering this Sunday, or send it to the church by mail. Alternatively, you may choose to make your commitment online at <u>(website address)</u>.

If you are receiving this letter and have already returned your card, please let us know by calling <u>(name)</u> at <u>(phone number)</u>.

I am so grateful for you and how you make the ministries of the church possible. Please feel free to call me at <u>(phone number)</u> if you have any questions. I'll see you in worship this weekend!

In Christ,

(Mailing #5: Responding Members)

Pledge Confirmation/Thank-You Letter

(date)

Dear (Name),

Thank you for sharing your estimate of giving with our church this year. You are an important part of the ministry of (church name) and of God's work in our community and the world. Through your gifts, you will be a part of changing the lives of children and youth, ministering to those in need, and welcoming others into the embrace of Christ.

Over the past few weeks, we've been looking at how we relate to our earthly possessions, how we make money and spend it, how we deal with debt, and how we live a life of gratitude no matter what we have. We've talked together about generosity, and we've seen that we can never have the life we want most—a life of joy—until we learn to give the gift of generosity.

Generosity changes us. We were created to be generous, and our generosity can be a great blessing in our lives. I pray that through your giving, you will find that blessings flow back into your life—blessings that you're not even expecting and that surprise you. I pray that you will find that your generosity changes the world as it changes one person at a time. This is prayer for you—and for our entire congregation.

My hope is that you will find yourself blessed as you experience joy in your generosity. Again, thank you for all that you do to make possible the ministry of our church. You make a difference here!

In Christ,

They are to do good, to be rich in good works, generous, and ready to share,
thus storing up for themselves the treasure of a good foundation for the future,
so that they may take hold of the life that really is life.
(1 Timothy 6:18-19)

(Mailing #5: Responding Members)

Bookmark

<u>Side One</u>

'Tis the gift to be simple, 'tis the gift to be free . . . —*19th-century Shaker song*

<u>(Side One can be art, a Bible verse, or your church name and address. In this example found under the Examples folder on your DVD-Rom, a verse from the Shaker song "Simple Gifts" is used.)</u>

<u>Side Two</u>

Thank you

Thank you for sharing your estimate of giving with our church this year. Your gifts are an act of worship and an investment in opportunities for God to work through us. Our prayer is that you will find greater contentment and simplicity in your life as you put God first in your giving and living and that you will experience the joy that comes from knowing our gifts honor God and change lives.

(Mailing #5: Non-responding Members / with return envelope)

Valued Member Survey

The purpose of this survey is to identify additional needs of the members of <u>(church name)</u>. We ask for your help with this important aspect of our ministry. Please check the correct answer for questions 1–3, and check all the relevant answers to question 4:

1. Are you a current member of <u>(church name)</u>? (YES___ NO___)
2. How many church services have you attended in the last 13 weeks? (6 or more___, 3 – 5___, 1 – 2___, None___)
3. In what groups at <u>(church name)</u> are you active? (Adult Sunday School___, Small Group___, DISCIPLE Bible Study___, Choir___, Other___, Not active in a group___), Other:_____
4. Please identify the factors that influenced your decision to not return a commitment card for <u>(calendar year)</u> (please check all items that influenced your decision):

    ___ My commitment card has been returned
    ___ I will continue to offer my financial support this year
    ___ Personal financial issues
    ___ Health issues
    ___ Personal issues in my family
    ___ Relocating
    ___ Became unemployed
    ___ Misplaced the commitment card or forgot
    ___ Unable to attend worship services
    ___ Have started attending another church
    ___ I will complete a commitment card next year
    ___ Concerns about the church
    ___ Felt the church did not respond to my needs
    ___ Did not feel a part of the church
    ___ Did not feel that my commitment was needed
    ___ Other (please describe)_____

    _____

Thank you for taking the time to share this information. Please return this survey by <u>(date)</u> using the enclosed postage-paid envelope, or place it in the offering plate in a worship service. Please do not sign this anonymous survey **unless you wish to update your membership records or desire a call from a minister of our church.** Survey results will help us better serve the congregation.

<u>(pastor's name and/or committee name)</u>

Caring Contact Calls Script
Enough Stewardship Campaign Follow-Up

Caller Name: _____ Date:_____

These calls are to be made to those who returned a commitment for (current calendar year) but have NOT for (next calendar year).

Step 1: Call and offer our concern.

"Hi, this is _____from (church name)'s Stewardship Campaign follow-up team."

"We are thankful for your financial and prayerful support of (church name)! We are calling because we received your commitment card for (current calendar year) last fall but for some reason we have not received your estimate of giving card for (next calendar year). (Name), are there any concerns, needs, or questions we might answer at this time?" (List on back of sheet.)

Step 2: Seek commitment.

"Will you be returning an estimate of giving card for (next calendar year)? Do you need for us to mail you a card, or would you prefer to fill out a card at the church and place it in the offering plate or make your commitment online?"
_____ Mail
_____ Card in offering plate
_____ Online

Step 3: Express appreciation.

"Thank you for your continued support of our ministries at (church name). Have a great day!"

Step 4: Pray with the person if he/she is experiencing problems/issues.

"Lord,
I lift up (Name) to you. Bless (Name) with the strength of your love. We thank you for our church family and pray for opportunities to support and encourage one another. In Christ's name, Amen."

Step 5: Evaluate the reception to your call.

On a scale of 1–10, with 10 being the best, how well do you think your call was received (from irritated to appreciated)?

_____

_____

_____

Thank you for serving in this telephone ministry!

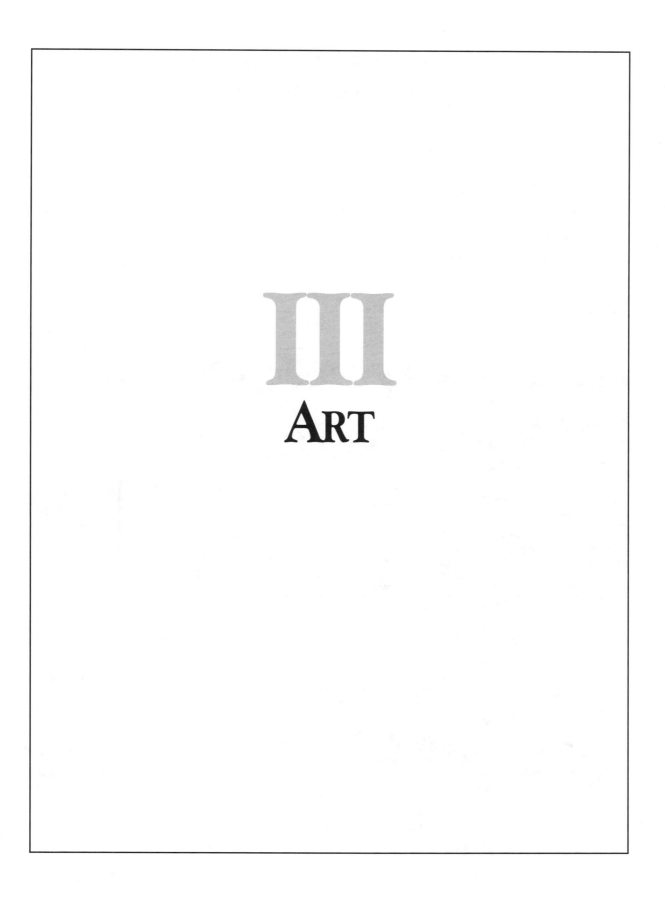

III
ART

ART IMAGES FOR CREATING YOUR OWN RESOURCES

During your campaign, you may want to design announcements, posters, postcards, letterhead, brochures, or other online or printed resources. On the DVD-Rom accompanying this book, in the Art folder, you will find art and image files that you can use for your own creations.

Images

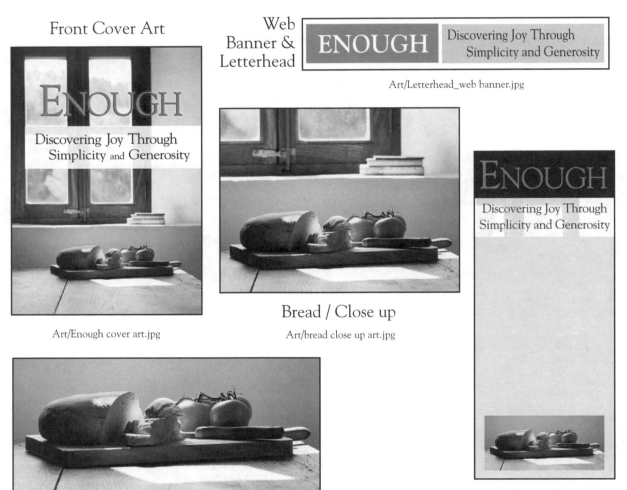

Front Cover Art

Art/Enough cover art.jpg

Web Banner & Letterhead

Art/Letterhead_web banner.jpg

Bread / Close up

Art/bread close up art.jpg

Vertical Art & PowerPoint

Art/Vertical art.jpg

Bread_No Window / Close up

Art/Bread-no window.jpg

There are files in jpg, tif, and pdf file formats. You'll find images of the *Enough* book cover, the window still life image from that cover, the background color, vertical art template, and *Enough* website banner/letterhead art that can be used on your website or to create stewardship campaign letterhead. Also on the DVD-Rom, in a folder titled Examples, you will see a few examples of how The United Methodist Church of the Resurrection (COR) designed their invitations, commitment cards, giving guides, and more.

On this page and the following page, you will find a thumbnail of each art image. File names are included for each of the COR example documents.

Examples

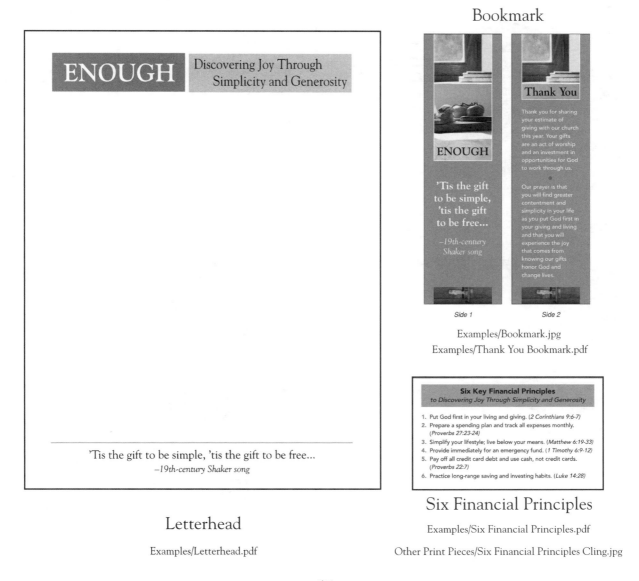

'Tis the gift to be simple, 'tis the gift to be free...
–19th-century Shaker song

Letterhead

Examples/Letterhead.pdf

Bookmark

Side 1   Side 2

Examples/Bookmark.jpg
Examples/Thank You Bookmark.pdf

Six Financial Principles

Examples/Six Financial Principles.pdf

Other Print Pieces/Six Financial Principles Cling.jpg

Examples

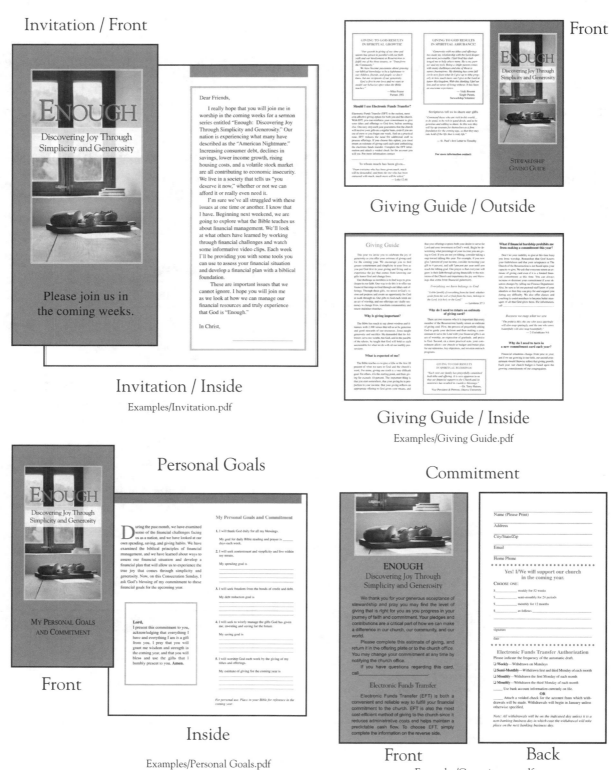

Invitation / Front

Invitation / Inside

Examples/Invitation.pdf

Front

Giving Guide / Outside

Giving Guide / Inside

Examples/Giving Guide.pdf

Personal Goals

Front

Inside

Examples/Personal Goals.pdf

Commitment

Front

Back

Examples/Commitment.pdf

IV
WORSHIP HELPS

WORSHIP HELPS

❑ Sermon Outlines
  - Optional Introductory Sermon: "Faith in the Midst of Financial Crisis"
  - Sermon #1: "When Dreams Become Nightmares"
  - Sermon #2: "Wisdom and Finance"
  - Sermon #3: "Cultivating Contentment"
  - Sermon #4: "Defined by Generosity"
❑ Video Clips
  - Using Video Clips in Worship
  - The Stock Market: 1941 to Today
  - The Economic Crisis
  - Finding Financial Stability
  - What Would You Take?
  - Tithing and the Ten Apples

OPTIONAL INTRODUCTORY SERMON: "FAITH IN THE MIDST OF FINANCIAL CRISIS" OUTLINE

The people who walked in darkness
*   have seen a great light;*
those who lived in a land of deep darkness—
*   on them light has shined. (Isaiah 9:2)*

I lift up my eyes to the hills—
*   from where will my help come?*
My help comes from the LORD,
*   who made heaven and earth. (Psalm 121:1-2)*

Command them not . . . to set their hope on the uncertainty of riches, but
rather on God. (1 Timothy 6:17)

I.   The Crisis of Faith

This is a remarkable and frightening time for our economy. The current economic crisis is also a crisis of faith. When we can't trust our financial institutions, the stock market, our banks, or our government we find ourselves afraid, and that fear often leads to either cynicism or panic. This may be the most potent enemy we're facing today. When the nation was in the midst of the Depression in 1933, Franklin Delano Roosevelt spoke these famous words in his first inaugural address:

> . . . Let me assert my firm belief that the only thing we have to fear is fear itself—nameless, unreasoning, unjustified terror which paralyzes needed efforts to convert retreat into advance. In every dark hour of our national life a leadership of frankness and vigor has met with that understanding and support of the people themselves which is essential to victory.
>
> (For full inaugural address: http://www.bartleby.com/124/pres49.html.)

II.   The Economic Reasons for Hope

It's not a question of "if" but "when" the stock market will recover. When we look at past market trends and identify those years when there was a significant drop, there always was a significant rise within a few years. (*Suggestion: Show the video clip "The Stock Market: 1941 to Today."*) While we wait for that rise, the economic reality is that some people may lose their jobs and others may lose their homes. Some may need to sell their cars because they can no longer afford the payments. Some may need help and support. Others will not feel the effects of the financial crisis at all. But we must not allow ourselves to be controlled by fear, because the Scriptures and our faith in God reassure us that we are going to be all right.

III.   Finding Faith in the Midst of Financial Crisis

At the center of the economic crisis is the extension and abuse of credit. *Credit* comes from the Latin word *credo*, which means, "I believe" or "I trust." To extend credit to someone is to believe or trust that he or she will repay. As Christians, our *credo* or trust is in God. The Apostle's Creed begins, "I believe (*credo*) in God the Father Almighty, maker of heaven and earth." Throughout the Bible we find words of hope and promise that remind us we have no reason to fear, for God is our refuge and strength:

- Isaiah 41:10
- Psalm 46:1-2
- Matthew 6:25, 33
- Matthew 14:27
- Philippians 4:6-7
- 1 Timothy 6:17
- Romans 8:37-39

IV. In Need of Salvation

The current economic crisis is a spiritual issue stemming from at least five of the seven deadly sins: gluttony, greed, sloth, envy, and pride. People are anxious all around us. We are to be beacons of hope and light. The church, the body of Christ, is to be a beacon of light inviting people to find deliverance, redemption, salvation, hope, and a new way of life.

Pastoral Prayer or Closing Prayer

"Faith in the Midst of Financial Crisis"

O God, we trust you with our lives. This world belongs to you. This earth is the Lord's and everything in it. We know the day will come, the Bible tells us in it's very final chapters, where everything we see and know will be destroyed and consumed by fire and there will be a new heaven and new earth. We remember how Paul sat in a prison cell, not afraid but boldly and courageously facing his death because he knew in whom he had believed. O God, we remember how the disciples saw Jesus walking on the water and they found courage when Jesus said to them, "I am here with you." And we remember how you promised you would never leave us or forsake us. O God, help us to be ambassadors of hope this week, bearing your light to others, helping them have a perspective on life, and helping them see you in us. Calm our anxious hearts. Help us to trust in you. Use this time to teach us, sanctify us, and perfect us. In your holy name, **Amen.**

Sermon #1: "When Dreams Become Nightmares" Outline

———————————

Some people, eager for money, have wandered from the faith, and pierced themselves with many griefs. (1 Timothy 6:10b, NIV)

The lover of money will not be satisfied with money; nor the lover of wealth, with gain. This also is vanity. (Ecclesiastes 5:10)

For what will it profit them if they gain the whole world but forfeit their life? Or what will they give in return for their life? (Matthew 16:26)

I. The American Dream

A. What Characterizes the Greatest Hopes, Desires, and Dreams of Most Americans?

For most people, the American Dream has to do with a subconscious desire for achieving success and satisfying the desire for material possessions. It is the opportunity to pursue more than what we have, to gain more than what we have, and to meet success. We tend to measure our success by the stuff that we possess.

B. The Pursuit of Immediate Material Pleasure

The love of money and the things money can buy is a primary or secondary motive behind most of what we Americans do. We want to consume, acquire, and buy our way to happiness—and we want it *now*. (*Suggestion: Show the video clip "The Economic Crisis."*)

II. The American Nightmare

The American Dream has become an American Nightmare due to two distinct yet related illnesses that impact us both socially and spiritually.

A. Affluenza

Affluenza is the constant need for more and bigger and better stuff—as well as the effect that this need has on us. It is the desire to acquire, and most of us have been infected by this virus to some degree.

- The average American home went from 1,660 square feet in 1973 to 2,400 square feet in 2004.
- Today there is estimated to be 1.9 billion square feet of self-storage space in America.[1]

B. Credit-itis

Credit-itis is an illness that is brought on by the opportunity to buy now and pay later, and it feeds on our desire for instant gratification. Our economy today is built on the concept of credit-itis. Unfortunately, it has exploited our lack of self-discipline and allowed us to feed our affluenza, wreaking havoc in our personal and national finances.

- Average credit card debt in America in 1990 was around $3,000. Today it's over $9,000.[2]
- The average sale is around 125 percent higher if we use a credit card than if we pay cash, because it doesn't feel real when we use plastic instead of cash.
- Credit-itis is not limited to purchases made with credit cards; it extends to car loans, mortgages, and other loans. The life of the average car loan and home mortgage continues to increase, while the average American's savings rate continues to decline.

III. The Deeper Problem Within

A. There Is a Spiritual Issue Beneath the Surface of Affluenza and Credit-itis

Our souls were created in the image of God, but they have been distorted. We were meant to desire God, but we have turned that desire toward possessions. We were meant to find our security in God, but we find it in amassing wealth. We were meant to love people, but instead we compete with them. We were meant to enjoy the simple pleasures of life, but we busy ourselves with pursuing money and things. We were meant to be generous and to share with those in need, but we selfishly hoard our resources for ourselves. There is a sin nature within us.

B. The Devil Plays Upon This Sin Nature

Jesus said, "The thief comes only to steal and kill and destroy. I came that they may have life, and have it abundantly" (John 10:10). The devil doesn't need to tempt us to do drugs or to steal or to have an extramarital affair in order to destroy us. All he needs to do is convince us to keep pursuing the American Dream—to keep up with the Joneses, borrow against our futures, enjoy more than we can afford, and indulge ourselves. By doing that, he will rob us of joy, make us slaves, and keep us from doing God's will.

- Matthew 4:8-10
- Luke 8:14
- Mark 8:36
- 1 Timothy 6:10

IV. The Bible's Solution

A. We Need a Heart Change

Although we receive a changed heart when we accept Christ, in a sense we need a heart change every morning. Each morning we should get down on our knees and say, "Lord, help me to be the person you want me to be *today*. Take away the desires that shouldn't be there, and help me be single-minded in my focus and my pursuit of you." As we do this, God comes and cleanses us from the inside out, purifying our hearts.

B. We Must Allow Christ to Work in Us

Christ works in us as we seek first his kingdom and strive to do his will. As this happens, we begin to sense a higher calling—a calling to simplicity and faithfulness and generosity. We begin to look at ways we can make a difference with our time and talents and resources. By pursuing good financial practices, we free ourselves from debt so that we are able to be in mission to the world. A key part of finding financial and spiritual freedom is found in simplicity and in exercising restraint. With the help of God, we can

- simplify our lives and silence the voices constantly telling us we need more
- live counter-culturally by living below, not above, our means
- build into our budgets the money to buy with cash instead of credit
- build into our budgets what we need to be able to live generously and faithfully

---

[1] "Self-storage Nation: Americans Are Storing More Stuff Than Ever," by Tom Vanderbilt, July 18, 2005; http://www.slate.com/id/2122832/.

[2] "Credit Card Debt Statistics," by Mark Brinker, August 2008; www.hoffmanbrinker.com/credit-card-debt-statistics.html.

Pastoral Prayer or Closing Prayer

"When Dreams Become Nightmares"

I'd like to invite you to put your hands on your lap, just extend your hands palm upright on your lap. And I would invite you to say this prayer with me, just quietly under your breath. Change my heart, oh God. Clean me out inside. Make me new. Heal my desires. Help me to hold my possessions loosely. Help me to love you. Teach me simplicity. Teach me generosity and help me have joy. I offer my life to you. In Jesus' name, **Amen.**

SERMON #2: "WISDOM AND FINANCE" OUTLINE

The plans of the diligent lead surely to abundance,
but everyone who is hasty comes only to want. (Proverbs 21:5)

Precious treasure remains in the house of the wise,
but the fool devours it. (Proverbs 21:20)

I. Where Did All Our Money Go?

A. Living as Prodigals

From Jesus' description in Luke 15:11-16, we see that the prodigal son had the habits of squandering and spending. The word *prodigal* does not mean someone who wanders away or is lost. It literally means "one who wastes money." A prodigal is one who wastes money, who is a spendthrift. Many of us struggle with that habit as well. We're not worried about tomorrow. We want it *today*. The problem with that kind of thinking is that, for most of us, the "famine" eventually comes. It comes when we have spent everything we have and even a little bit of next year's income. So we use the credit card and charge it, and we go a little further into debt. Finally, we come to a place where we "find ourselves." We have nothing left, not even any credit, and we can't figure out how we are we going to make it.

B. The More We Make, the More We Waste

It seems that the more financially secure we become, the less we worry about spending money here and there. We waste a dollar on this or that, and we forget where it went. Money just seems to flow through our fingers. We're not as careful with our money as we should be. There are many ways we waste money, but there are two primary money-wasters that many of us struggle with. It is not necessary to eliminate these two things all together, but we should think more carefully about how we spend our money.

1. Impulse buying.

Tips for avoiding impulse buying:

- Never go grocery shopping when you are hungry.
- Shop for what you need only.
- Make a list and stick to it; buy what you need and get out of the store!
- Wait twenty-four hours before purchasing an impulse buy.

2. Eating out.

The issue is frequency. The average American eats out an average of four times a week.[3] By eating out less frequently, we will have more money to save, spend on something more important, or give away.

II.   Clarifying Our Relationship With Money and Possessions

We do not exist simply to consume as much as we can and get as much pleasure as we can while we are here on this earth. We have a higher purpose. We need to know and understand our life purpose—our vision or mission or calling—and then spend our money in ways that are consistent with this purpose or calling.

A. Be Clear About Your Purpose and Calling

Our society tells us that our life purpose is to consume—to make as much money as possible and to blow as much money as possible. The Bible tells us that we were created to care for God's creation. We were created to love God and to love our neighbors as ourselves. We were created to care for our families and those in need. We were created to glorify God, to seek justice, and to do mercy. Our money and possessions should be devoted to helping us fulfill this calling. We are to use our resources to help care for our families and others—to serve Christ and the world through the church, missions, and everyday opportunities. We have a life purpose that is greater than our own self-interests, and how we spend our God-given resources reflects our understanding and commitment to this life purpose or mission.

B. Set Worthy Goals

Being able to accomplish the greater purposes God has for our lives requires some measure of planning. Taking the time to set goals related to our lives and our finances is crucial if we are to become wise stewards of our God-given resources. Each of us should think about our life purpose and goals and then identify two short-term financial goals, two mid-range financial goals, and two long-term financial goals that are aimed at helping us to accomplish our broader life goals. At least one goal in each category should relate specifically to our faith. (*Suggestion: Use the bulletin insert "My Life and Financial Goals Worksheet."*)

III. The Discipline of Managing Your Money

A. The Necessity of a Budget/Spending Plan

Once we have set some financial goals, we need to develop a plan to meet those goals. A budget is a spending plan that enables us to accomplish our goals. Some people use an envelope system to help them manage their saving and spending and stay on budget. Others use a variety of different approaches. Many people find it helpful to seek the advice of a financial advisor. For those who find themselves in the midst of a financial crisis, a financial counselor can help to work out terms with creditors and develop a workable financial plan. Whatever approach you choose, the important thing is simply to have a plan. (*Suggestion: Show the video clip "Finding Financial Stability."*)

B. Six Financial Planning Principles

The following financial planning principles can help us to manage our money with wisdom and faith:

1. Pay your tithe and offering first.

Put God first in your living and your giving. Give your tithe and offering from the "top" of your paycheck, and then live on whatever remains.

2. Create a budget and track your expenses.

Creating a budget is simply developing a plan in which you tell your money what you want it to do. Tracking your expenses with a budget is like getting on the scales: It allows you to see how you are doing and motivates you to be more careful with your expenditures. (*Suggestion: Use the bulletin insert "Basic Budget Worksheet."*)

3. Simplify your lifestyle (live below your means).

Because this discipline is critical to the success of any financial plan, next Sunday's sermon will be devoted to this topic.

4. Establish an emergency fund.

An emergency fund is an account separate from checking or long-term savings that is set aside specifically for emergencies. Dave Ramsey recommends beginning with $1,000 and building that to three months' worth of income.[4] When you have this amount, you won't need to use your credit cards anymore.

5. Pay off your credit cards, use cash/debit cards for purchases, and use credit wisely.

As you are building your emergency fund, begin to pay off your credit card debt and start using cash or debit cards for purchases. Some experts suggest starting with the credit card that has the highest interest rate. Others suggest paying down the smallest debt first, experiencing that victory, and applying your payments from the first card to the second, and so on, creating a snowball effect to pay off the cards as soon as possible. Cut up your cards as you pay them down so that you are not trapped or leveraged by your future for present-day pleasure, as the prodigal son was. If you must use a credit card, such as when traveling or making purchases online, be sure to pay off the debt monthly. If you are unable to do this, then it is better for you to cut up your cards and stop using them altogether.

6. Practice long-term savings and investing habits.

Saving money is the number-one wise money management principle everyone should practice. We do not save merely for the sake of saving. There is a word for that: hoarding. Hoarding is frowned upon in the Bible as the practice of fools and those who fail to understand the purpose of life. Saving, on the other hand, is meant to be purposeful. There are three types of savings we should have: 1) emergency savings; 2) savings for wants and goals; and 3) retirement savings.

Resources for Developing a Budget
http://www.crown.org/Tools/Calculators/Budgeting_SpendingPlan.asp

This is a fun and helpful budgeting calculator that automatically generates a suggested budget based upon the user's inputs and Crown's recommended expenditures.

http://crowncanada.ca/resources/CrownSpendingPlan2.pdf

This is another Crown resources site focused on budgeting and financial freedom. There is good information here.

Getting Out of Debt

Dave Ramsey's Financial Peace University offers a great deal of online information including his approach to reducing debt found at this site: **www.daveramsey.com/the_truth_about/get_out_of_debt_4055.html.cfm**

---

3 "Statistics About Eating Dinner Out," by Magali Rheault, *Kiplinger's Personal Finance Magazine*, October 2000; http://findarticles.com/p/articles/mi_m1318/is_10_54/ai_65368848?tag=content;col1.
4 *The Total Money Makeover*, by Dave Ramsey (Thomas Nelson, 2007); pp. 102–08.

Pastoral Prayer or Closing Prayer

"Wisdom and Finance"

God, you know what we don't even know. We don't know where every dime went, but somehow you know what we did with all that we had, last year and the year before that. You don't forbid us from having joy in our possessions. In fact, you delight in having joy for us. But what you know is that just acquiring more and more stuff isn't where we find joy. Lord, forgive us for being wasteful, for being prodigals. Forgive us for leveraging our future in order to have pleasure in the present. And help us to be good managers of the talents that you've given to us. Help us to be generous and willing to share, kingdom-minded and focused on accomplishing your purposes for our lives. In Jesus' name, **Amen.**

Sermon #3: "Cultivating Contentment" Outline

Keep your lives free from the love of money, and be content with what you have; for he has said, "I will never leave you or forsake you." So we can say with confidence, "The Lord is my helper; I will not be afraid." (Hebrews 13:5-6)

And [Jesus] said to them, "Take care! Be on your guard against all kinds of greed; for one's life does not consist in the abundance of possessions." (Luke 12:15)

Whatever my eyes desired I did not keep from them; I kept my heart from no pleasure. . . . Then I considered all that my hands had done and the toil I had spent in doing it, and again, all was vanity and a chasing after wind. (Ecclesiastes 2:10-11)

Introduction

In recent years we have witnessed a number of devastating natural disasters, including hurricanes, floods, tornadoes, and wildfires. Natural disasters remind us that everything in this world is temporary. This is why we can say with Jesus, "[My] life does not consist in the abundance of possessions" (Luke 12:15). Yet the culture is shouting that it's not true. The result is a wrestling in our hearts. Despite the fact that we say we believe Jesus' words, we still find ourselves devoting a great deal of our time, talents, and resources to the acquisition of more stuff. We *say* that our lives do not consist in the abundance of our possessions, but we *live* as if they do.

I. Restless Heart Syndrome – Struggling With Discontent

Perhaps you've heard of restless legs syndrome (RLS), a condition in which one has twitches and contractions in the legs. Restless Heart Syndrome (RHS) works in a similar way, but in the heart—or soul. Its primary symptom is discontent. We find that we are never satisfied with anything. The moment we acquire something, we scarcely take time to enjoy it before we want something else. We are perennially discontent.

A. When Discontentment Is a Virtue

There is a certain discontent that God intended us to have. God actually wired our hearts so that they would be discontent with certain things, causing us to seek the only One who can fully satisfy us. We are meant to yearn to know God more, to cultivate a deeper prayer life, to pursue justice and holiness with increasing fervor, to love others more, and to grow in grace and character and wisdom with each passing day.

B. When Discontentment Destroys

The problem is that those things we should be content with are the very things we find ourselves hopelessly discontented with. For example, we find ourselves discontented with our stuff, our jobs, our churches, our children, and our spouses. God must look down on us and feel the way we feel when we give someone we really care for a special gift and he or she asks for the gift receipt. It's as if we're saying to God, "I don't like what you have given me, God; and I want to trade it in and get something better than what you gave me."

II. Four Keys to Cultivating Contentment

The Apostle Paul is an excellent example of contentment. In his letter to the Philippians, he wrote of the "secret" to his contentment (Philippians 4:11-12). Like Paul, we can learn to be content in whatever circumstances we may find ourselves. Four keys, which include the "secret" Paul referred to in his letter, can help us to do that.

A. Four Words to Repeat: *It Could Be Worse*

John Ortberg, pastor at Menlo Park Presbyterian Church in California, says there are four words we should say whenever we find ourselves discontented with something or someone: "It could be worse." This is essentially the practice of looking on the bright side or finding the silver lining. It is recognizing that no matter what we may not like about a thing or person or circumstance, we can always find something good to focus on if only we will choose to do so.

B. One Question to Ask: *For How Long Will This Make Me Happy?*

So often we buy something, thinking it will make us happy, only to find that the happiness lasts about as long as it takes to open the box. There is a moment of satisfaction when we make the purchase, but the item does not continue to bring satisfaction over a period of time. Many of the things we buy are simply not worth the expense. This is why it is a good idea to try before you buy.

C. Developing a Grateful Heart

Gratitude is essential if we are to be content. The Apostle Paul said that we are to "give thanks in all circumstances" (1 Thessalonians 5:18). A grateful heart recognizes that all of life is a gift. Contentment comes when we spend more time giving thanks for what we have than thinking about what's missing or wrong in our lives.

D. Where Does Your Soul Find True Satisfaction?

The world answers this question by telling us that we find satisfaction in ease and luxury and comfort and money. The Bible, however, answers the question very differently. From Genesis to Revelation, it tells us that we find our satisfaction in God alone.

- "Thou hast made us for thyself, O Lord, and our hearts are restless until they find their rest in thee." (Saint Augustine)
- "O God, you are my God, I seek you, / my soul thirsts for you. . . . / My soul is satisfied as with a rich feast, / and my mouth praises you with joyful lips / when I think of you on my bed, / and meditate on you in the watches of the night." (Psalm 63:1, 6)
- "Whatever my eyes desired I did not keep from them; I kept my heart from no pleasure. . . . Then I considered all that my hands had done and the toil I had spent in doing it, and again, all was vanity and a chasing after wind." (Ecclesiastes 2:10-11)
- Jesus said the two most important things we must do are to "love the Lord your God with all your heart, and with all your soul, and with all your mind,"

and to "love your neighbor as yourself" (Matthew 22:37, 39). If we keep our focus on these two things, we will find satisfaction for our souls and lasting contentment.

III. Five Steps for Simplifying Our Lives

In addition to cultivating contentment in our lives, we need to cultivate simplicity. Contentment and simplicity go hand in hand.

A. Set a Goal of Reducing Your Consumption, and Live Below Your Means

Set a tangible goal to reduce your own personal consumption and the production of waste in your life. For example, use canvas bags when you go grocery shopping and refuse any extra packaging. Whenever you are making purchases, look at the mid-grade instead of the top-of-the-line product. When buying a new car, aim to improve fuel economy over your existing car by at least 10 percent. Reduce your utilities by 10 percent by setting the thermostat back a couple of degrees when you are away during the day and asleep at night. Find other ways to reduce your consumption and live below your means. Do some research, share ideas with others, or have a brainstorming session with your family.

B. Before Making a Purchase, Ask Yourself: *Do I Really Need This?* and, *Why Do I Want This?*

These questions will help you to determine the true motivation of your desired purchase. Is it a need, a self-esteem issue, or something else? You may find yourself wrestling with your true motive and decide that your reason for purchasing the item is not a good one.

C. Use Something Up Before Buying Something New

Take good care of the things you buy and use them until they are empty, broken, or worn out. Buy things that are made to last; and, when buying things that have a short lifespan, spend your money wisely.

D. Plan Low-cost Entertainment That Enriches

When it comes to choosing entertainment for your family or friends, plan things that are simple and cheap. You'll be amazed at how much more pleasure you derive from low-cost, simple activities.

E. Ask Yourself: *Are There Major Changes That Would Allow Me to Simplify My Life?*

Consider selling a car and buying one you pay for in full, downsizing your home, or getting rid of a club membership you don't use. Ask yourself questions related to your home, possessions, job, and activities to identify some significant changes that will simplify your life. Remember, if you cannot do all the things God is calling you to do and you're unable to find joy in your life, perhaps it's time to simplify in some major ways.

IV. The Power of Self-Control

Simplifying your life requires the practice of self-control. Solomon wrote, "Like a city whose walls are broken down / is a [person] who lacks self-control" (Proverbs 25:28, NIV). When a city's walls are broken through, the enemy can march right in and destroy it. There is no longer any protection. Likewise, self-control is a wall around your heart and life that protects you from yourself, from temptation, and from sins that are deadly and ultimately can destroy you. Self-control comes down to making a choice between satisfying an impulse to gain instant gratification and choosing not to act upon the opportunity for instant gratification for some higher cause or greater gratification later. Self-control is about forgoing instant gratification by stopping to think about the answers to three questions:

- "What are the long-term consequences of this action?"
- "Is there a higher good or a better outcome if I used this resource of time, money, or energy in another way?"
- "Will this action honor God?"

V. Conclusion: Which Tent Will You Live In?

Will you live in discon-**tent** or con-**tent**-ment? You and you alone determine which "tent" will be yours. You choose it in large part by deciding what life is about. If you decide that "life does not consist in the abundance of your possessions," then you are choosing contentment. Choosing contentment means we look to God as our Source, giving thanks for what we have; we ask God to give us the right perspective on money and possessions and to change our hearts each day; we decide to live simpler lives, wasting less and conserving more; and we choose to give more generously. *(Suggestion: Watch the video clip "What Would You Take?"*

Pastoral Prayer or Closing Prayer

"Cultivating Contentment"

Lord, we pray that you might cure us of Restless Heart Syndrome. And we are truly sorry for the times that we received the gifts that you give to us and asked for the gift receipt, unsatisfied with the person you entrusted to our care, unsatisfied with our children or our parents, unsatisfied with our home and our car, our healthcare and our jobs. God forgive us for the times we've offended you by our discontent. Forgive us for being content with the things we were not supposed to be content with. Help us have a hunger and a deep longing to pursue righteousness and holiness and justice and love, to long for you and for your will for our lives. Help us in this. Help us to simplify, to get off the treadmill, the hamster wheel, and to find in you our peace. We ask these mercies in your holy name, **Amen.**

Sermon #4: "Defined by Generosity" Outline

As for those who in the present age are rich, command them not to be haughty, or to set their hopes on the uncertainty of riches, but rather on God who richly provides us with everything for our enjoyment. They are to do good, to be rich in good works, generous, and ready to share, thus storing up for themselves the treasure of a good foundation for the future, so that they may take hold of the life that really is life. (1 Timothy 6:17-19)

Some give freely, yet grow all the richer;
*   others withhold what is due, and only suffer want.*
A generous person will be enriched,
*   and one who gives water will get water. (Proverbs 11:24-25)*

Those who are generous are blessed,
*   for they share their bread with the poor. (Proverbs 22:9)*

I.   A Theological Foundation for a Generous Life

A. Created to Be Generous; Tempted to Hoard

God created us with the willingness to give—to God and to others. This design is part of our makeup; we actually have the *need* to be generous. Yet there are two voices that "war" against our God-given impulse toward generosity, tempting us to keep or hoard what we have.

1. The voice of fear.

Fear of what might happen to us, along with a misplaced idea about the true source of our security, keeps us from being generous and leads us to hoard what we have. The truth is that hoarding offers us no real security in this world.

2. The voice of self-gratification.

Our culture tells us that our lives consist in the abundance of our possessions and pleasurable experiences. So we find ourselves thinking, *If I give, there won't be enough left for me.*

B. Defeating the Voices

When we give our lives to Christ, invite him to be Lord, and allow the Holy Spirit to begin changing us from the inside out, we find that our fears begin to dissipate and our aim in life shifts from seeking personal pleasure to pleasing God and caring for others. Although we still may wrestle with the voices from time to time, we are able to silence them more readily and effectively the more we grow in Christ. And the more we grow in Christ, realizing that our lives belong to him, the more generous we become. Generosity is a fruit of spiritual growth.

C. Biblical Reasons to Give to God and Others

- We find more joy in doing things for other people and for God than we ever did in doing things for ourselves. (Acts 20:35)
- In the very act of losing our lives, we find life. (Matthew 16:25)
- Life is a gift, and everything belongs to God. (Psalm 24:1; Leviticus 25:23)

D. Biblical Guidelines for Giving

From the early days of the Old Testament, God's people observed the practice of giving some portion of the best of what they had to God. A gift offered to God was called the *first fruits* or the *tithe*, and it equaled one-tenth of one's flocks or crops or income. Abraham was the first to give a tithe or tenth.

- Genesis 14:20b
- Genesis 28:18-22
- Leviticus 27:30-33

1. Giving a tithe.

As Christians who live under the new covenant, we are not bound by the Law of Moses; we look to it as a guide. Yet most Christians agree that the tithe is a good guideline for our lives, and one that is pleasing to God. (*Suggestion: Use the video clip "Tithing and the Ten Apples."*) Though tithing can be a struggle, it is possible at virtually every income level. If you cannot tithe right away, take a step in that direction. Perhaps you can give 2 percent or 5 percent or 7 percent. God understands where you are, and God will help you make the adjustments necessary for you to become more and more generous.

2. Giving beyond the tithe.

Tithing is a floor, not a ceiling. God calls us to grow beyond the tithe. We should strive to set aside an additional percentage of our income as offerings for other things that are important to us, such as mission projects, schools, church building funds, and other nonprofit organizations.

II.   What Our Giving Means to God

A. How Does Our Giving Affect God?

From the earliest biblical times, the primary way people worshipped God was by building an altar and offering the fruit of one's labors upon it to God. They would burn the sacrifice of an animal or grain as a way of expressing their gratitude, devotion, and desire to honor God. The scent of the offering was said to be pleasing to God. It wasn't that God loved the smell of burnt meat and grain. Rather, God saw that people were giving a gift that expressed love, faith, and the desire to please and honor God; and this moved God's heart. When given in this spirit, our offerings bless the Lord.

B. What is God's response to our giving?
- Luke 6:38
- Matthew 25:14-30

III.   How Our Generosity Affects Us

A. Through It Our Hearts Are Changed

When we are generous—to God and to our families, friends, neighbors, and others who are in need—our hearts are filled with joy. They are enlarged by the very act of giving. When we give generously, we become more generous.

B. In It We Find the Blessings of God (Malachi 3:10)

Many Christians have it wrong. They say that if you give, then God will give more back to you. But that is not how it works. We do not give to God so that we can get something in return. The amazing thing is that when we give to God and to others, the blessings just seem to come back to us. Of course, there is no guarantee that if you tithe you will never lose your job or never have other bad things happen to you. Nevertheless, when we give generously, the unmistakable blessings of God flow into our lives. *(Suggestion: Insert the Personal Goals and Commitment card in the bulletin and use it at the end of the sermon. Have a time of silent meditation and prayer, inviting everyone to complete a card at this time.)*

Pastoral Prayer or Closing Prayer

"Defined by Generosity"

Oh God, we thank you that you have given us life, that you sustain us by the power of your Holy Spirit and that you gave Jesus Christ as an offering for us and for our sins. We thank you for the abundance that we have in our lives. And we pray that you would help us. Help us, oh Lord, to honor you with our tithes. Help us to care for the poor and those who are in need. Help us to recognize that it is more blessed to give than to receive. We offer ourselves to you. Guide us now as we prepare to fill out our commitment cards. Help us, oh Lord, to do your will. Lead us, we pray. In your holy name, **Amen.**

USING VIDEO CLIPS IN WORSHIP

During the *Simplicity, Generosity, and Joy* sermon series at The Church of the Resurrection—which led to the *Enough* study and stewardship resources—graphics, props, and video interviews were used to highlight the main points of the content. Because of the appeal and effectiveness of using video clips in worship, we have included several videos on the accompanying DVD. In this section you will find an outline for each video that provides an introduction, a transcript of the video, and a possible closing.

You and your worship leaders can use the videos in several ways. The clips may be useful as ideas and inspiration for planning your own worship services. You may find that some of the clips will serve well as promotions for the series. Show them in the weeks prior to the launch of your campaign and/or upload them to your church website. The clips also can be played in worship as part of the sermon. Each individual video on the DVD plays without an opening graphic, music, or closing credits so that it will flow right into the service. You'll notice that each video starts with a couple of seconds of black screen to make queuing the clip easier for the person running the equipment.

The video clips are listed below, along with a sermon recommendation for each. Please note that the DVD introduction by Adam Hamilton, "Introduction" (5 minutes, 55 seconds), is a particularly effective introduction to the campaign. Those clips with asterisks are excerpts from sermons preached at The Church of the Resurrection that are included on the *Enough: Discovering Joy Through Simplicity and Generosity* study DVD.

The Stock Market: 1941 to Today *
Introductory Sermon: Faith in the Midst of Financial Crisis

The Economic Crisis
Sermon #1: When Dreams Become Nightmares

Finding Financial Stability
Sermon #2: Wisdom and Finance

What Would You Take? *
Sermon #3: Cultivating Contentment

Tithing and the Ten Apples *
Sermon #4: Defined by Generosity

THE STOCK MARKET: 1941 TO TODAY

Running Time: 1 minute, 44 seconds
Speaker: Adam Hamilton from his sermon, *"Faith in the Midst of Financial Crisis"*
(Recommended for use with the Introductory Sermon by the same title)

In this short clip, Adam presents a light and hopeful look at the history of the Dow Jones index. Using a logarithmic chart of the index from 1941 through 2007, he tracks the ups and downs and recoveries seen in the market.

Possible introduction:

Now, I'm not an economist, but this week, I've been reading essays from all sides—from a variety of viewpoints. We may not know which of the approaches to recovery is the most promising, but I am convinced that we will survive a downturn in our economy. We have before, and we will do it again. Let's take a look at what the stock market has done since about World War II.

Transcript:

Now the concerns in the economy are broader than the stock market. But the stock market is like gas prices. It's a number we can watch and somehow, even if we don't fully understand it and I'm guessing most of us don't fully understand what the Dow Jones average represents—we know it represents something important; and so we see the numbers go up or down and that sort of does something to our psyches.

You've seen charts like this but this is a chart of the stock market... the Dow Jones Industrial Average from 1941 to 2007. If you invested $1,000 in 1941, by the end of 2007 it was worth $1,731,000. Now today, it's worth $1,100,000 dollars because of the drop in the market. But a million, one hundred thousand, still. So we look at this and if you look at this, the chart shows what the Dow has done during a World War, during the Cold War, during the Korean War, what it did when a president of the United States was assassinated. What it did when one [president] resigned in the Watergate crisis and in the midst of Vietnam. What happened when the stock market crashed at various points in the past . . . the first World Trade Center bombing. The second World Trade Center 9/11 attack, the Iraq War, and you see the trend of this. And this is part of the reason why folks out there who aren't panicked are going, "Alright, I wonder when do I put money back in the market"; because here's what happens within 3 to 5 years of a huge downturn like this the market has exceeded where it was before. So, people are wondering, "When do I get back in so I can take advantage of what's going on?" I'm not trying to give you advice on the stock market, what I'm trying to say is if you take it in historical perspective, our country is not going to fall apart in the next year, or two years, or three years. So, part of what we have to have in the middle of this [crisis] when we start to feel fear and panic is just a bit of historical perspective.

Possible closing:

Now, that's a look at the big picture. I know there are people who are immediately affected—for whom even a short-term downturn is a problem—those with kids in college depending on funds they've invested, retired folks who are living on those investments, and certainly people who have lost their jobs. But we are going to come through this. We'll look for ways to surround each other with support and help one another through those times. But we'll get through.

THE ECONOMIC CRISIS

Running Time: 1 minute, 51 seconds
Speakers: Dr. William Black, Associate Professor of Economics
and Law University of Missouri - Kansas City
Dr. Stephen Pruitt, Arven Gottleib/Missouri Endowed
Chair of Business, Economics and Finance,
Henry Bloch School of Business and Public Administration
University of Missouri - Kansas City
(Recommended for use with Sermon #1: *"When Dreams Become
Nightmares"* or in the optional introductory sermon,
"Faith in the Midst of Financial Crisis")

Possible introduction:

We've talked about how our desire for more, more than we need and more than we can afford, has fueled individual financial disasters. This style of living and consuming has become an American way of life. Let's listen to a couple of economists to see how these same human vulnerabilities have affected the larger markets and the current crisis and even why our keenest economic advisors didn't fully see this latest crisis coming. What part has human nature played?

Transcript:

Dr. Black: We forgot about a whole bunch of things about human beings and human behavior and about human susceptibility to doing things wrong. In Greenspan's recent testimony in front of Congress, that was essentially his mea culpa . . . I forgot human nature. . . . The average American has made himself vulnerable to this and by borrowing way, way, way too much . . . not close to the line, but enormously over the line compared to everything we know about human history and so this had to end badly. . . . We have repeatedly failed the ethical and market test and if we want to remain a great nation, we really have to start reconsidering things. And the best way to reconsider them is frankly, go back to a lot of old stuff, not new stuff . . . the stuff that you were taught in your church.

Dr. Pruitt: It's the inability so much of this problem, is the inability to delay gratification. I guess that's the number one problem that humanity faces . . . we just want it. . . . There is a saving grace . . . perhaps faith can take us into ways that we can fight this way of inevitable human nature that will be with us on this side of heaven. That we don't go out and follow our baser instincts. . . . Maybe, just maybe, we can just sit back and say I can resist temptation too and live slightly different lives than we did in the past.

Possible closing:

Over the next few weeks we are going to explore that question—how can our faith help us overcome our natures and help us life the lives God planned for us. We're going to look at what the Bible says about wise and prudent use of our money, how we begin to find contentment in simpler living, tips so that we don't feel that need for immediate gratification grabbing our soul all the time. And then the last week we're gonna talk about a real key to this, and that's generosity.

FINDING FINANCIAL STABILITY

———

Running Time: 1 minute, 20 seconds
Speaker: Lee Ann Carter, Parthenon Credit Union,
Chief Operating Officer
(Recommended for use with Sermon #2: *"Wisdom and Finance"*)

In this short, practical piece, Lee Ann Carter describes four simple steps that are critical to financial health and stability: tracking spending, setting a budget with specific goals, paying off debt, and saving.

Possible introduction:

Your money is entrusted to you. You're called to manage it well. And God will hold each of us accountable in the end for what we do with our time, our talents, and our resources. And so we begin to think, *How can we help each other have good financial practices?* We asked a credit union manager to share with us some of the basic things she tells her members about how to be good financial managers. As you watch this short video clip, listen for four basic things. You know them already, but often we fail to practice them. Take a listen:

Transcript:

We found over the past few years that many people were living beyond their means and didn't really grasp what was happening. They're juggling payments, maybe paying bills with one credit card to save cash to pay down another card, maybe making only minimum payments on any of their credit cards. Their total personal debt was rising—compounded by some pretty significant interest rates. So, how do you get out of this?

The first thing you have to do is track your spending. Where is the money going every week? Most of us don't know how much we're spending at the grocery store or in restaurants every month. Take a good look at this picture—and then you must set some financial goals. That is the foundation of every budget or every financial plan. What do you want to achieve ... by when? The next is pay off your debt. It is the best way to simplify your life. Use your credit wisely. If you want something, save up to get it. And, then the absolute number-one thing that everybody needs to be doing is create a savings account. Take it directly out of your paycheck. Don't see it. Have it go into an account. I know you know these things. Just like you know you need to exercise and eat right. The challenge is making a plan and sticking with it.

Possible closing:

I know you know these things, too. The hard part is doing this on a daily basis. Let's encourage us to have healthy financial habits. So to try to help you with that, we've given you a little tool inside your bulletin. And if you'd take this out, it says, "Six Key Financial Principles" ...

What Would You Take?

————————————

Running Time: 2 minutes, 11 seconds
Speaker: Adam Hamilton from his sermon, *"Cultivating Contentment"*
(Recommended for use with Sermon #3 by the same title)

In this multimedia clip, Adam Hamilton recounts the news coverage of the 2007 California wildfires and the belongings evacuees chose to take as they fled the fires. It works well as a sermon opening or closing.

Possible introduction:

Are there major changes that would allow you to simplify your life? Are you living a lifestyle you can't afford? Driving a car or paying a mortgage that is pushing you beyond your means? I want to encourage you if you feel this stress and it's keeping you from doing the things God is calling you to do, maybe it's time to simplify in the major things.

Benjamin Franklin had it right when he said this: "Contentment makes poor men rich, but discontentment makes rich men poor." I'd rather you be someone who is poor but who has contentment than someone who had everything and doesn't even realize it. What is really important in your life? Let's take a look at this video—what is really important to you?

Transcript:

All right, well, Jesus told us that our life does not consist in the abundance of our possessions. And every once in a while we finally see that and we get it. I mean, most of the time the media is telling us that's not true. But every once in a while the media says that's right. That happened this week in southern California. When we were watching the news and we were seeing wildfires come and consume people's entire neighborhoods.

There were a million people who were displaced for a period of time. And there were people like one family—in the middle of the night, their daughter had awakened them. They woke up and they smelled the smell of smoke. They looked out their back windows and they watched as the fire leapt [across] the interstate and was coming up the hill behind their house with the winds blowing it towards them. It was racing toward their house. They realized they had this much time to get out. They had grabbed their children. They grabbed just a few things. They ran out to the car and escaped just before the flames engulfed a portion of their home and all of their neighbors' homes. And people came back and nothing was there. It was all gone. And suddenly you become aware: My life does not consist in the abundance of my possession.

Time magazine went to Qualcom Stadium and they began to just talk to people who had ten minutes or less to escape their homes, [asking,] *What did you take with you?*[5] And I thought you might find this interesting. I mean, what would you take with you? This little boy, his name is Andrew, he saved his pillow. Of all the important possessions, it was his pillow. And this woman, Shirvy, she saved two photographs and a childhood book by Dr. Seuss. There was Angel. He saved a saxophone. He'd just started playing sax. And Karen, she saved her two cats. And Michelle? She saved her shoes, her purse. She saved her high school diploma and she saved her Bible. She saved her Bible. What would you save … if the tornado were coming and you knew it was going to hit your house and it'd be a direct hit, and you're running to the basement shelter, what is it you're gonna grab? And … you already know this intuitively. You know … you know none of that stuff in the end really matters. You know that when you die all pictures and all the videos and all that other stuff you collected is going in the garbage or maybe going to be sold at a garage sale by your kids or your grandkids. Was it worth it, and how long will it take you to learn that your life does not consist in the abundance of your possessions? I want to invite us to learn that lesson and to live like it.

Possible closing:

So, I remind you once more of these words from the Shaker hymn,

'Tis the gift to be simple, 'tis the gift to be free.
'Tis the gift to come down where we ought to be;
And when we find ourselves in the place just right,
'Twill be in a valley of love and delight.

When true simplicity is gain'd,
To bow and to bend we shan't be asham'd,
To turn, turn will be our delight,
Til by turning, turning we come out right.

Let's pray together.

---

[5] "What They Saved From the Fire" photo essay, *Time* magazine; http://www.time.com/time/photo-gallery/0,29307,1675264 _1472476,00.html.

TITHING AND THE TEN APPLES

Running Time: 2 minutes, 49 seconds
Speaker: Adam Hamilton from his sermon, *"Defined by Generosity"*
(Recommended for use with Sermon #4 by the same title)

In this clip, which can be shown or recreated, Adam Hamilton uses ten apples as an example of our possessions.

Possible introduction:

We've looked at tithing in the Old Testament. But what does God expect of us today? Most of us Christians look back at the Old Testament tithe and say we think that's still a guide for our lives—a guide for what God would ask of us. And that tenth goes to accomplish the work of God's kingdom through the church. And the church, then, is responsible for praying and discerning. The lay people who are in charge of our church's finances are responsible for asking, "What does God want to do through us in the next year—through the resources that you have committed to God?" Yet even though we think the tithe is a good guide, it's a challenge. Let's take a look at a video that brings this point home. [Or go straight into a live demonstration.]

Transcript:

Now when it comes to this idea of tithing it's … a challenging idea for many of us. I mean, it's a stretch, especially when you first start becoming a Christian and you're having those impulses, that war that's going on inside you between fear and the desire for pleasure. Give a tenth? You've got to be kidding. Now David Slagle, who's a pastor in Atlanta, had a wonderful, graphic way [to illustrate] how God sees this. And so I wanted to share that with you. God sees it—sort of your wealth and your income—like these ten apples that I have before me. And God says nine of these are yours. Use them to take care of your family, to clothe yourselves. Use them for food and for shelter and set some of [them] aside for retirement and give some away to your friends and some are designed to be used for the poor and for pleasure and for trips and vacations.

You've got nine of these apples. But the Lord says, "One of them is mine. And it's meant to be used, first of all, as a way for you to express your praise and your love for me—your obedience and devotion. But then I'm going to use it to accomplish my purposes in the world."

But here's what happens with many of us. Many of us find—because the society is pulling us in so many directions—that nine apples aren't enough anymore. I mean, they really aren't. How can we do all the fun stuff and the cool stuff and the stuff we need to do and pay the bills and everything on just nine apples? And so we think, "Well the Lord's not going to mind if we just take a little bit." You know, there's a trip that we've been wanting to take. And it's really important and it's a special trip. And we're just going to take just take a little bit of the Lord's apple. He'll understand. And then it's Christmastime and we didn't set anything aside for all these Christmas presents. And we need people to know, and it's kind of giving. It's not to God, but it is to other people. It's to our children and others and so [God will] understand. We'll take a little more of [God's] apple.

And start thinking about retirement. It's coming up sooner than you think. And you know, I need to be setting aside more in retirement. But I can't stop spending from these apples. I've got to take that from somewhere else. And [I need them for] medical emergencies because we didn't set aside emergency funds in our savings account. And it's time to get a new car. And then there's that big screen right before the Super Bowl we've been thinking about getting—and the new house. You know, our old house doesn't really satisfy us anymore and so there's that. And pretty soon there's not much left—I mean, from the Lord's apple. Wait a minute. Hold on. And then we say, "Well, Lord, this is your part. I'm going to give that to you."

Possible closing:

That is a graphic and humorous portrayal of what we know can happen in many of our lives. The pressures and distractions begin to consume us. By the time we get around to God, there is not much left. And we may even take one last bite before we offer it to God.

LEADERS AND
SMALL GROUPS

INVOLVING THE CONGREGATION IN STUDY

One of the best ways to take the *Enough* Stewardship Campaign beyond an annual stewardship drive to a transformational experience resulting in spiritual growth and financial health—on both a personal and congregational level—is through small-group study. Encourage Sunday school classes, as well as Wednesday night groups and other groups meeting at various times during the week, to read and study the book *Enough* during the campaign emphasis. This four- or five-week study with video and leader guide will engage participants in group discussion and walk them through both group and personal application exercises related to each of the worship themes:

Faith in the Midst of Financial Crisis (Optional Introduction)
When Dreams Become Nightmares (Week 1)
Wisdom and Finance (Week 2)
Cultivating Contentment (Week 3)
Defined by Generosity (Week 4)

Together in group study, class members will have the opportunity for more in-depth study on each of the sermon topics, they will gain greater understanding of core concepts, as well as establish a "support system" and accountability group for the weeks ahead as they implement the spiritual and financial principles and strategies outlined in the study/campaign.

At its core, individual reading with deep personal reflection is critical to experiencing transformation as an individual and as a community. The sermons, articles, and video excerpts all create meaningful conversations but present only a portion of the message. The book *Enough* presents the full message with Scripture, a deeper consideration of each topic, more example stories, and simple financial that help each individual or household begin to thoughtfully consider daily habits, choices, and lifestyles.

In an ideal program, each adult class and each household would read *Enough: Discovering Joy Through Simplicity and Generosity* together during the series. Work with Cokesbury or your local bookstore for quantity discounts that will allow broad participation in the message of simplicity and generosity. A deep personal exploration of this message, in community and individually, will produce long-range, life-changing transformation.

An Overview of *Enough*: Discovering Joy Through Simplicity and Generosity Excerpted From the DVD Leader Guide

---

Enough is a video-based study that explores what the Bible teaches us about financial management. Its purpose is to help participants get off the consumerism treadmill and find the joy and contentment that come with a simpler and more generous way of living. Participants will assess their financial situation and develop a financial plan with a biblical foundation. This four-week study is appropriate for Sunday school classes, study groups, and others desiring to become wise stewards of the resources God has given them. As group leader, your role will be to facilitate the weekly sessions using the book *Enough*, the video DVD, and the accompanying leader guide.

A Quick Overview

Because no two groups are alike, the leader guide for *Enough* is designed to give you flexibility and choice in tailoring the sessions for your group. You may choose one of the following format options, or adapt these as you wish to meet the schedule and needs of your particular group. (Note: The times indicated within parentheses are merely estimates. You may move at a faster or slower pace, making adjustments as necessary to stay on schedule.)

Basic Option: 60 minutes
Opening Prayer (2 minutes)
Biblical Foundation (3 minutes)
Video Presentation (15 minutes)
Group Discussion (30 minutes)
Taking It to Heart This Week (5 minutes)
Closing Prayer (<5 minutes)

Extended Option: 90 minutes
Opening Prayer (2 minutes)
Biblical Foundation (3 minutes)
Opening Activity (10–15 minutes)
Video Presentation (15 minutes)
Group Discussion (30 minutes)
Group Activity (15 minutes)
Taking It to Heart This Week (5 minutes)
Closing Prayer (<5 minutes)

Although you are encouraged to adapt the sessions to meet your needs, you also are encouraged to make prayer and Scripture regular components of the weekly group sessions. Feel free to use the opening and closing prayers provided or create your own prayers. In either case, the intent is to "cover" the group session in prayer, acknowledging that we are incapable of becoming wise stewards of our resources apart from God's grace and help. Likewise, the Scripture verses provided for each group session are intended to provide a biblical foundation for the group session as well as for participants' continuing reflection and application during the week.

In addition to the components outlined above, the following "leader helps" are provided to equip you for each group session:

Main Idea (session theme)
Session Goals (objectives for the group session)
Key Insights (summary of main points from the video)
Leader Extra (additional information related to the topic)
Notable Quote (noteworthy quote from the video)

You may use these helps for your personal preparation only, or you may choose to incorporate them into the group session in some way. For example, you might choose to write the main idea and/or session goals on a board or chart prior to the beginning of class, review the key insights from the video either before or after group discussion, incorporate the leader extra into group discussion, and close with the notable quote.

In addition to the materials provided for each group session, you will find a reproducible participant handout at the end of each session. This handout includes a summary of the key insights from the video as well as "Taking It to Heart This Week" application exercises for the coming week. Remind participants that these exercises are designed to help them get the most out of this study that they possibly can. They alone are the ones who will determine whether or not this is just another group study or a transformational experience that will have a lasting, positive impact on their lives.

An optional introductory session with video is provided as an engaging way to begin the study. This will extend the study from four to five weeks. Should you choose not to hold an introductory session, you may elect to view the introductory video during the group session for Week 1. (Note: You will need an additional 14 minutes for viewing the introductory video; another option is to omit one of the activities or shorten the group discussion.)

Finally, there is a bonus video segment, "To Be a Blessing," that covers the story of Jeff Hanson (see pp. 89–91 in *Enough*). If you choose to view this during the group session for Week 4, you will need an additional 5 minutes.

Helpful Hints

Here are a few helpful hints to help you prepare for and lead the weekly group sessions.

- Become familiar with the material before the group session. If possible, watch the DVD segment in advance.
- Choose the various components you will use during the group session, including the specific discussion questions you plan to cover. (Highlight these or put a checkmark beside them.) Remember, you do not have to use all of the questions provided, and you even can create your own.
- Secure a TV and DVD player in advance; oversee room setup.
- Be enthusiastic. Remember, you set the tone for the class.
- Create a climate of participation, encouraging individuals to participate as they feel comfortable.
- Communicate the importance of group discussions and group exercises.
- To stimulate group discussion, consider reviewing the key insights first and then asking participants to tell what they saw as the highlights of the video.
- If no one answers at first, don't be afraid of a little silence. Count to seven

silently; then say something such as, "Would anyone like to go first?" If no one responds, venture an answer yourself. Then ask for comments and other responses.

- Model openness as you share with the group. Group members will follow your example. If you share at a surface level, everyone else will follow suit.
- Draw out participants without asking them to share what they are unwilling to share. Make eye contact with someone and say something such as, "How about someone else?"
- Encourage multiple answers or responses before moving on.
- Ask "Why?" or "Why do you believe that?" to help continue a discussion and give it greater depth.
- Affirm others' responses with comments such as, "Great" or "Thanks" or "Good insight"—especially if this is the first time someone has spoken during the group session.
- Give everyone a chance to talk, but keep the conversation moving. Moderate to prevent a few individuals from doing all the talking.
- Monitor your own contributions. If you are doing most of the talking, back off so that you do not train the group to not respond.
- Remember that you do not have to have all the answers. Your job is to keep the discussion going and encourage participation.
- Honor the time schedule. If a session is running longer than expected, get consensus from the group before continuing beyond the agreed upon time.
- Consider involving group members in various aspects of the group session, such as asking for volunteers to run the DVD, read the prayers or say their own, read the Scripture, and so forth.

Above all, remember to pray. Pray for God to prepare and guide you, pray for your group members by name and for whatever God may do in their hearts and lives, and pray for God's presence and leading before each session. Prayer will both encourage and empower you for the weeks ahead.

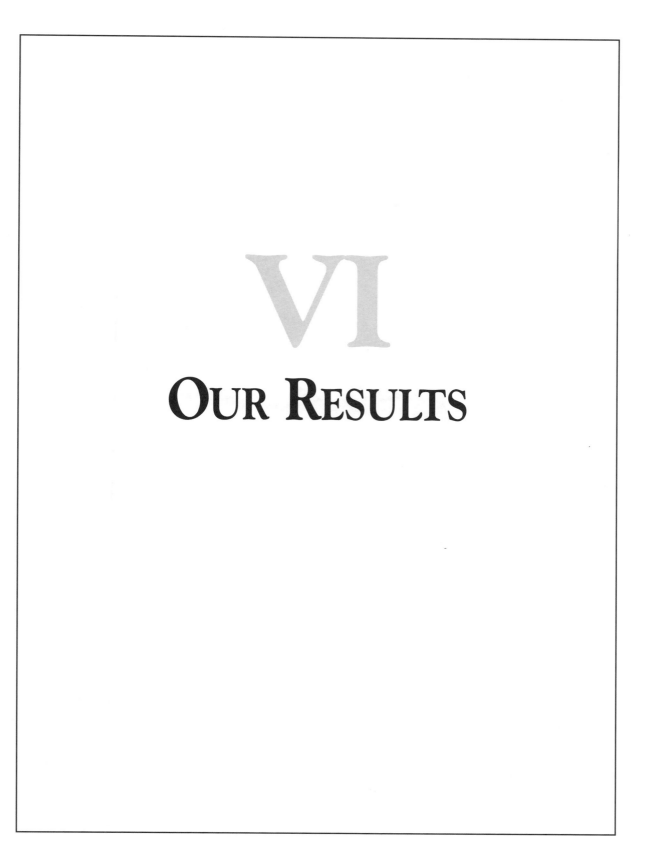

VI

OUR RESULTS

OUR RESULTS

Response to the Stewardship Campaign

    The normal campaigns at The Church of the Resurrection would seem very familiar to most pastors and staff. In a typical campaign we teach about tithing, generosity, and stewardship. I typically preach two sermons during the campaigns, and we include video testimonials of people who have grown to become tithers. We include print pieces and highlight the accomplishments of the last year and the visions we will be pursuing in the next year. We have a follow-up phase for those who did not turn in their commitment cards in an attempt to encourage everyone to return their card. Even when the campaign is inspiring, and the best it could be, attendance often drops significantly during this two- to three-week time period. And in recent years, the percentage of our members turning in commitment cards has been steadily declining. (The amount of overall giving was increasing, but the number of people returning cards was decreasing, a trend seen in many churches across the country.)

    In 2007, in light of what we could see were real problems that people were having with money—not just with our own members, but nationally—we decided to scrap the stewardship campaign we had planned. We felt that what was needed was not a fundraising campaign, but a series of sermons and a campaign that was more pastoral in nature. We needed to acknowledge the problems Americans have in our relationship with money: overspending, maxed-out credit cards, plummeting savings rates, and a lifestyle that is unsustainable. The series did not have a tone of chastisement, but of confession and a desire to help. We struck a note with our membership and community. Attendance actually went up during this series. People invited their friends. Those in the community sensed that this series was what they needed. We were surprised by the enthusiastic response to small, practical helps like the key tag and the cling with the Six Key Financial Principles. Our team felt that the response came because we identified a real problem and spoke together frankly about it, offering practical helps and a clear biblical message.

We knew that we still needed to invite people to make their financial commitments and to speak about giving, but we would talk about this as one of several important components to a healthy and biblical approach to money. Our lives are meant to be characterized both by simplicity and generosity, and both of these lead to joy.

Performance in Giving

The increase in participation in the commitments was dramatic. In 2005, our total percentage of members returning commitment cards was 56 percent. At that point some were suggesting we stop asking people to turn in commitment cards completely, noting that the national trend was moving away from this. But I felt that commitment cards are important. They lead people to rethink their giving for the coming year. And persons who fill out a commitment card have, in our experience, been more likely to fulfill this commitment than those whose commitment is internal, but never written down.

By the end of the *Simplicity, Generosity, and Joy* series we had a larger number of members return pledge cards than ever before. Our total pledged giving was up 10 percent. The percentage of people who returned a commitment card rose from 56 percent to 64 percent. But perhaps most surprising of all for us was their faithfulness in giving in 2008.

In a typical year we anticipate receiving 92.5 percent of what was actually pledged by our members. We build our budget upon this number, plus another 18 percent from nonpledged giving. In 2008, even after the economic downturn, we received over 97 percent of what was pledged by our members, which, with the nonpledged giving, led to a significant surplus over budget. (This helped sustain us in 2009 as the economy continued to falter.)

We were able to build upon this effort in our November 2008 campaign called *Reset* where we looked at how Americans need to reset their spending and financial practices, given the new economic realities we live within. In that effort we saw the number of pledge cards returned increase again, to over 72 percent. While the average commitment fell due to the number of our members who had lost jobs, we invited those who had lost jobs to return a card indicating this, and indicating that, while their pledge may be $0, they will pray and serve and give when they obtain another job. At Church of the Resurrection, we give a coffee mug to every person who turns in a commitment card each year as a way of expressing thanks; we give these mugs to persons whose commitment is $0, as well, recognizing their pledge to give as they are able.

Lasting Results

The work we did together as a congregation continues to be reflected in our people, their lives, and their giving patterns. After the first campaign, we increased the number of financial management workshops we offered our members and the community. In cooperation with Dave Ramsey and Financial Peace University, we distributed audio CDs to 3,500 families resulting in 750 people taking the course. We've offered other courses and mentoring from financial experts in our own congregation. It's been an ongoing time of learning and change.

While many large churches across the country have experienced significant decreases in giving and in their budgets as a result of the economic recession, our giving as of the writing of this guide in April 2009 is up over 2008, despite the increased number of people out of work in our congregation. We believe this is a direct result of helping people realign their priorities while cultivating better financial practices.

Our prayer for you is that you and your entire congregation will be blessed as individuals and households find contentment and true joy, and that each of us and each of you continue to grow deeper in faith.

MORE RESOURCES

ENOUGH RESOURCES

If you or your congregation or small group would like to know more about the *Enough* message and available products to support your stewardship program, please visit AbingdonPress.com for more information. Each of the items below are described in the *Enough* Stewardship Campaign series and are readily available.

Enough: Discovering Joy Through Simplicity and Generosity
This original book is suggested for individuals and small groups and forms the basis for the sermon series, DVD, and program.

9781426702334

$10

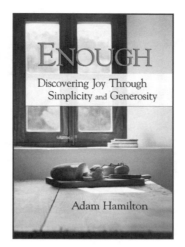

***Enough: Discovering Joy Through Simplicity and Generosity* DVD**. This DVD includes five video sessions for small-group use, each between 14 and 18 minutes in length. A 56-page leader guide with session outlines, opening and closing prayers, activities, and group discussion questions is included.

843504004606

$39.00

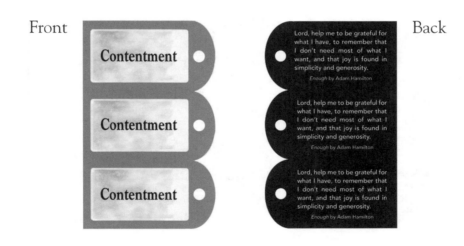

Front   Back

Enough Contentment Key Tags – Identical to the Contentment Key Tags that are included with every copy of *Enough: Discovering Joy Through Simplicity and Generosity*, these unique key tags remind us daily of the importance of being grateful and that true joy is found in generosity and simplicity.

9781426706110

$18.00 Package of 90

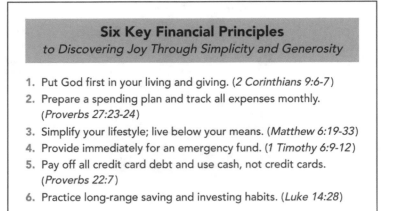

Six Key Financial Principles
to Discovering Joy Through Simplicity and Generosity

1. Put God first in your living and giving. (*2 Corinthians 9:6-7*)
2. Prepare a spending plan and track all expenses monthly. (*Proverbs 27:23-24*)
3. Simplify your lifestyle; live below your means. (*Matthew 6:19-33*)
4. Provide immediately for an emergency fund. (*1 Timothy 6:9-12*)
5. Pay off all credit card debt and use cash, not credit cards. (*Proverbs 22:7*)
6. Practice long-range saving and investing habits. (*Luke 14:28*)

Enough Six Key Financial Principles Static Cling – These 5 inch x 3 inch static clings list the Six Key Financial Principles. They are perfect for displaying on a mirror or window that you see every day, such as a bathroom mirror or your back door window, to remind you of the six essential steps to discovering joy through simplicity and generosity.

9781426706103
$14.00 Package of 50

Side 1   Side 2

Enough Thank-You Bookmarks – These 2 inch x 7 inch bookmarks are an effective (and cost effective) thank-you and acknowledgment of any level of pledge commitment.

9781426706127
$4.00 Package of 25

OUR *ENOUGH* STEWARDSHIP CAMPAIGN TEAM

Name	Contact Phone/Email	Responsible For

OUR *ENOUGH* STEWARDSHIP CAMPAIGN ACTIVITY SCHEDULE

Please refer to pages 15–18 in this *Enough* Stewardship Campaign Program Guide for a more complete description of the Activity Schedule. It will help keep your campaign on track in the coming weeks. If you like, jot down your key target dates here.

Key Dates

Planning (Month _____)

Goal Date: _____

- Planning and Budget Review/Approval
- Order Copies of Enough: Discovering Joy Through Simplicity and Generosity and Enough: Discovering Joy Through Simplicity and Generosity DVD with Leader Guide for Small Groups
- Order additional items (bookmarks, clings, key tags, thank-you gifts)
- Other:_____

Getting Started (Month _____)

    Weeks 1–2 _____: Upload introductory materials to website.

    Week 3 _____: Distribute Enough books and DVD with Leader Guide.

    Week 4 _____: Small-group study begins. Mailing #1 sent out.

Campaign is Underway (Month _____)

    Week 1: _____: Upload Sermon, Email, and Bulletin to website. Mailing #2 goes out. Small-group study begins with Session #1.

Week 2: _____: Upload Sermon, Email, Bulletin Article, and Bulletin Inserts to website. Distribute Six Key Financial Principles cling. Small-group study meets.

Week 3: _____: Upload Sermon, Email, and Bulletin Article to website. Distribute Six Key Financial Principles cling. Small-group study meets.

Week 4: _____: Upload Sermon, Email, and Pledging tools to website. Mailing #3 goes out. Small-group study meets.

Consecration & Celebration Sundays (Month _____)

Week 1: _____: First Consecration Sunday. Distribute additional commitment cards. Distribute thank-you gifts.

Week 2: _____: Second Consecration Sunday. Distribute additional commitment cards.

Week 3: _____: Follow-up Caring Contact Calls begin.

Week 4: _____: Celebration Sunday. Share results of the stewardship campaign.

Follow-up (Month _____)

Week 1: _____: Valued Member Survey mailed to non-responding members.

OUR *ENOUGH* STEWARDSHIP CAMPAIGN
THINGS TO DO LIST

WHAT YOU'LL FIND ON THE DVD-ROM

The enclosed DVD-Rom includes all the full text and art for the worship helps, letters, announcements and examples described and shown within this guide plus five short video clips for use in worship including:

1. The Stock Market: 1941 to Today (1:44)
2. The Economic Crisis (1:51)
3. Finding Financial Stability (1:20)
4. What Would You Take? (2:11)
5. Tithing and the Ten Apples (2:49)

Using the DVD as a computer DVD-Rom, you'll find the following folders with these additional resources.

Art: Art files that can be used to create your own promotional material, letterhead, mailers, and web designs.

Articles, Emails, and Inserts: Bulletin announcements and inserts, emails from the pastor, and a newsletter article.

Examples: Full color examples of the mailings and commitment cards used at The United Methodist Church of the Resurrection.

Letters: Customizable Microsoft Word documents for each letter used in the campaign.

Other Print Pieces: Text from other pieces including the campaign invitation, giving guide, and more.

Post Campaign Follow-up: Helpful follow-ups including a letter to non-responding members, follow-up contact calls, and a membership survey.

PowerPoint Slides: Five different color slide templates for use in worship.

Sermons: Full sermon outlines for each sermon in the series and helps for incorporating the worship videos.

PowerPoint Slides Quick Start

1. Put the DVD-Rom in your computer DVD drive.

2. Open PowerPoint on your computer and choose "File," "Open," and then choose the PowerPoint file from the DVD.

3. Select one of the PowerPoint slide files that you like. After you open the file, go ahead and save it to your own computer (using "Save As").

4. Add your own text and titles to the text boxes.

5. To reorder your slide show, choose "View" and "Slide Sorter." Here you can drag slides and drop them in the order that you want.

Troubleshooting With PowerPoint Slide Shows

1. Problems saving your work? Use "Save As" under the "File" to save a copy on your computer. The DVD-Rom is a read-only file. You can't save any new material on any of the DVDs.

2. To add more slides to your slide show, choose "Insert" from the menu and then "new slide." If you like the slide with the shaded box and would like more of this slide format, you can go to that slide and choose "Insert" and "Duplicate Slide." An identical slide will be added to your show.

3. To reorder your slide show, choose "View" and then "Slide Sorter" from the menu. In this mode, you can drag the slides into the order you want. To go back to the normal view, choose "View" and "Normal."

4. If you'd like to add an image, choose "Insert" from the menu, and then "Picture" and "From File." If you choose from your DVD, you can add an image, like the cover of *Enough: Discovering Joy Through Simplicity and Generosity*, to your slide.

5. Remember to save your finished slide show, choose "File," "Save As," and save the file on your computer or a disk.